Nectar of Nondual Truth

CONTENTS

10 Shmita: A Year of Letting Go
by Rabbi Rami Shapiro
Let it go, let it be, and realize the beingness of beings — this is the essence of the subtle and little known, rarely practiced principle of Shmita — which Rabbi Rami asks us to consider well and rrspond to.

12 New Dispensation & Neo-Vedanta
by Babaji Bob Kindler
A major part of spiritual awakening today must include fresh awareness around the auspicious visitation of the Kali Yuga Avatar and His prime messenger to the earth plane. What they brought to us is invaluable.

21 A Universal Perspective
by Rev. Chris VonLobedan
With the advent of recent luminaries onto the earth plane comes a re-envisioning and reworking of old religious perspectives, brought about by souls who are moving swiftly towards a deeper understanding of the Universality of all religions.

23 Turning Within
by Swami Brahmeshananda
Statements like "Go within," and, "The Kingdom of Heaven lies within," are not mere suggestions to be considered lightly and discarded. An actual inner life is based upon the mind's withdrawal from externals like objects, pleasures, and worlds of all types, and a dedicated taking of refuge in the Eternal Reality that transcends both inner and outer considerations.

29 An Interview with Dudjom Rinpoche
by Lex Hixon
When traditions such as Tibetan Buddhism came here to the West, the people of these regions saw that separating good and bad thoughts was not just a matter of therapeutical psychology and external counseling, but needed the attendance of holding a spiritual Ideal combined with daily practice in order to be effective for any real and abiding transformation of mind.

32 When the Great Swami was Among Us
by Annapurna Sarada
The questions who were we then?, how far have we come?, and who are we today?, get asked in this deep article, all in the context of Swami Vivekananda's two visits in the late 1800's and early 1900's.

39 Godblogs and Brahman Bytes, (cont.)
by Babaji Bob Kindler
The special sayings and poignant spiritual stories of Sri Ramakrishna and other luminaries are taken up again, to hone the subtle sensibilites of our inner sight.

41 Two Aspects of Reality
by Swami Sunirmalananda
To clarify terms such as Vedanta and Advaita, Brahman and Atman, Nirguna and Saguna, so as to illumine our understanding in Vedanta Philosophy, is the point of this enriching offering.

43 Empowering Language with Wisdom
by Brother Tadrupa
Wisdom words have the potential to transform lives, and depending upon the perspective the individual takes, can do away with ignorance and lift the soul into higher levels of realized consciousness.

46 Understanding Islam
by Sheikh Nur Al Jerrahi
This reprint of an article on Lex Hixon in his important role as leader of the Western branch of the Jerrahi Order of Sufis, has been taken from Nectar Issue #19, 2005.

50 Discrimination Between the Absolute & the Relative
by SRV Staff
With the considerable aid of dharma teachings, illumined teachers, and the revelation of nonduality, the true Goal of human existence can be attained. Vedanta answers all questions that the sincere aspirant might have in its quest for clarity, revealing the line of demarcation between what can be accepted and what needs to be rejected along the well-marked out pathway to Enlightenment.

"....as Sri Ramakrishna has put it, not all rivers reach the ocean. Some go underground prior to that merging, others end in a lake rather than the sea. Some even dry up along their course. In this way, the many religious traditions of the world appeal to different groups of souls, the individuals of which are at various levels of understanding."

Publisher's Page

Sarada Ramakrishna Vivekananda – SRV Associations
"Setting the feet of humanity on the path of Universal Truth."

Notes on an Advaitic Journal

At the basis of Advaita as the philosophy of Shankara and his gurus, there is Advaita as experience. Advaita as experience represents that supreme place where all diversity merges in its Essence. It is not combatant or immiscible with qualified or dualistic approaches, but rather provides them their place of consummate arrival. Where actual practice rather than mere book learning is emphasized, where religion, philosophy and spirituality are not separate from one another, where knowledge and love, reason and devotion, are never divorced from each other, there does the truth of authentic nonduality effloresce.

Historically speaking, experiential Advaita originated with the ancient Rishis. Therefore, the Upanisads contain the nondual truths of the Vedas which declare: idam mahabhutam anantam aparam vijnanaghana eva, "This great Being is endless and without limit. It is a mass of indivisible Consciousness only."

SRV Associations & Universality

The SRV Associations are part of a worldwide movement of spiritual aspirants devoted to the study and practice of Vedanta and Divine Mother Wisdom. The ideals of this ancient pathway to God, exemplified in the lives of Sri Sarada Devi, Sri Ramakrishna and Swami Vivekananda, are the original and eternal perfection of the Soul and its inherent oneness with Reality, the manifesting of divinity in our lives, selfless service of all beings as God, and reverence for the ultimate unity of all sacred traditions. To this end our purpose is to study, worship, and contemplate Truth so that spirituality may flourish. This is the Advaitic way — "None else but Self, none other than Mother."

Nectar's Mission — Advaita-Satya-Amritam

In Sanskrit, amrita, nectar also means Immortality – and this is, indeed, what we are offering: opportunities to become aware of this Amrita that is our very Essence via the rarefied teachings from Vedanta and the World Religions and Philosophies that appear in each issue of Nectar.

Nectar of Non-Dual Truth is SRV Associations' heartfelt offering of highest Wisdom to the human community. It is the sincerest form of love and service we know to disseminate non-dual Truth and teachings which transmit pure knowledge, pure love, and true universality. Through Nectar we are working out SRV's mission of spiritual upliftment and education. Please join us; this is a universal movement.

Keeping Nectar in Print

Subscribe to Nectar of Non-Dual Truth

Since 2009, Nectar has been a free/donation-based instrument of Universal Religious & Philosophical Teachings. Unfortunately, postage and printing has far exceeded donations for many years. Thus, we must return to subscriptions to stay in print. Please subscribe to Nectar using the form at the back of this issue.

You Can Help Others Receive Nectar

We continue to supply free copies to prison inmates, religious organizations, and low income persons in the U.S. You can help bridge the financial gap with a separate donation to Nectar. SRV Associations is a 501(c)3 tax-exempt organization.

To donate online, Visit: www.srv.org > Giving. To donate by check, mail to: SRV Associations, PO Box 1364, Honokaa, HI 96727 (payable to: SRV Associations)

808-990-3354 | srvinfo@srv.org | www.srv.org

With reverent gratitude, we heartily thank the contributing writers of this issue of Nectar of Nondual Truth, who have so graciously and selflessly shared the wisdom of their respective traditions and practices.

Staff of Nectar of Nondual Truth

Publisher
Sarada Ramakrishna Vivekananda Associations
* an Annual Publication

For more information concerning the SRV Associations or Nectar of Nondual Truth please contact:
SRV Associations, PO Box 1364, Honoka'a, HI 96727
Phone: (808) 990-3354
e-mail: srvinfo@srv.org   website: www.srv.org
Nectar Subscription is on a donation basis only

No part of this publication may be reproduced or transmitted in any form without permission from the publisher. Entire contents copyright 2022. All Rights Reserved. ISSN 1531-1414

Editor
Babaji Bob Kindler

Associate Editor
Annapurna Sarada

Production
Lokelani Kindler

Cover Image:
Photo by Babaji

Acknowledgement
Image of Ramakrishna's Disciples
Courtesy of Vedanta Press
800-816-2242

Contributing Writers
Swami Brahmeshananda
Swami Sunirmalananda
Sheikh Nur Al Jerrahi
Rev. Chris VonLobedan
Rabbi Rami Shapiro
Annapurna Sarada
Brother Tadrupa
Alexander Hixon
Babaji Bob Kindler

EDITORIAL

In Nectar of Nondual Truth's 37th issue, dating back to 2001, the ongoing examination of the connections between true religion and liberating philosophy, as well as the adept separation of the ego from the Great Self, goes forth. For, the ego has two powers, one that obscures Truth and the other that seems to distort It. When the soul begins to see clearly due to the intense practice of time-tested methods, the revelatory power begins to ripen the human ego. Purification leading to transformation ending in transcendence describes the process at these higher levels of Awareness.

As the articles of this issue of Nectar are taken up, imbibed, and studied, it becomes evident that all the world's religions are seeking this positive end, but are using various means to accomplish it. However, as Sri Ramakrishna has put it, not all rivers reach the ocean. Some go underground prior to that merging, others end in a lake rather than the sea. Some even dry up along their course. In this way, the many religious traditions of the world appeal to different groups of souls, the individuals of who are at various levels of understanding. This is why devotion may be the accented route for certain religions and seekers, wisdom for others, and meditation for still others. It may even be that the path of work and action takes the fore, as in this day and age.

And so, even though Nectar of Nondual Truth focuses on advaita, or nonduality, that highest existence gets approached through qualified paths, through simultaneously existing lineages, through utilizing a host of yogas. In this issue, Vedanta, Tibetan Buddhism, Christianity, and Judaism find themselves side by side for consideration — not to vie with one another for supremacy, but rather to share perspectives with a view to do away with unclarity and unveil the Truth at various levels. An open-minded stance based in Universality will be required, and is the fresh way cited by perfected beings living in these very times, along with the rest of us.

Thus, if Nectar of Nondual Truth is the only, or one of the few journals in print, that offers forth a multitude of religious views, all without bias, encouraging practitioners to both explore the religions of the One God and urging them to enter into the practice of them, the time has come for many more seekers to open up and do so. Using the same analogy, this is rather like the voyager who utilizes different waterways in order to reach the ocean. He does not dislike the water in one river and like the water in the next, but courses along, navigating each river in turn, observing their respective properties and directions. As the Prasna Upanisad states in this regard:

"Where is that Purusha? Here within this body exists that Purusha, from which rise the 16 kalas (prana, faith, 5 elements, senses, mind, food, virility, austerity, mantras, sacrifice, worlds, names/forms). As flowing rivers reach the ocean and merge, and people near to the ocean then speak of the ocean alone, so too do these kalas disappear into the Purusha, and seers speak of the Purusha alone. Knowing all this, death cannot hurt them, and they tell us, 'I know only of the Supreme Brahman; there is nothing higher than that.'"

Similarly, universally-minded beings, as they study in various traditions, soon become aware of Brahman only, by whatever name it is called by each religion. To know the Mind of God is to know the religious traditions and be able to comprehend their teachings. As the Upanisads of India, often called the Mother of all Religions, state:

"May we always and ever be,
Like mighty rivers flowing into the sea,
Losing all sense of name, form, and identity,
Into the Ocean of Absolute Reality."

Om Peace, Peace, Peace

Babaji Bob Kindler

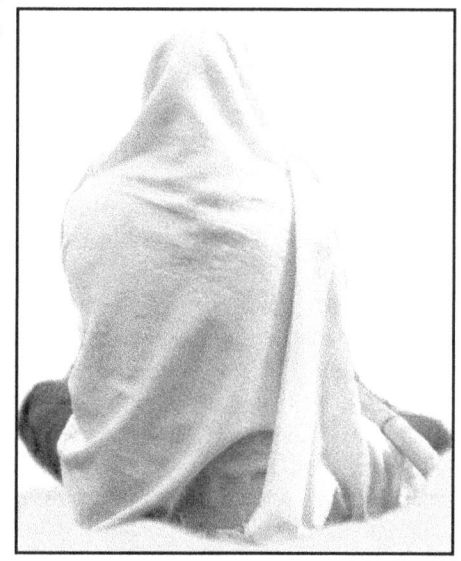

NECTAR OF ADVAITIC INSTRUCTION

Questions from Our Readers

For sincere seekers, profound questions often come bubbling up from the depths of the yearning heart and seeking mind. The Lord, Himself, takes these up through the presence of multiple gurus, acharyas, and luminaries who maintain a position on earth within the physical body, to fulfill the soul and return It to Its source.

"When studying, it seems like vasanas have a 'partner like' role, in that samskaras created and reinforced by the kleshas lead to more vasanas, which then feed into more samskaras resulting in more tickets on this transmigration roller coaster. It seems like if one can utilize kriya-yoga and viveka-dhyana, one can create samskaras that are not of the nature of the kleshas, thus purifying the vasanas in the mind or rendering the mind nir-vasana. Does this line of reasoning follow the tradition/teachings?"

Yes, your reasoning and connections, on all of these points, make good sense, and hit the mark. Yoga is a vast system, most effective when utilized traditionally with guru and scriptures. Keep receiving the lessons, questioning about them, then dive in for more input over an extended period of time. Soon you will be facile with the system, and answers will come to you swiftly and spontaneously.

"I was listening to readings on Swami Vivekananda today, and he was talking about weakness, and extolling the virtues of the householder, and what kind of fearlessness one needs. Suffice to say, my proverbial tail was between my legs as I listened. Lately, I feel like I've been failing a few of my duties as a householder. Something happened today at work that really caused me to step back and look at my own conduct, and my perception of what I think is right and good, and what is actually right and good, from multiple stations: the idea of renunciate and householder, the accurate understanding of manifestations of Brahman, my relationship with people in general. I believe the mantra is dredging up some buried things but the positive note is that I can at least address them and change my course for the better. So my question: How to affirm I am liberated at this moment? I've tried looking in the mirror and saying "You are liberated!" but perhaps there's more to it than that! Is it more of a repetitive affirmation that dawns on the mind over time, or will the mantra start to implant this idea in my conscious awareness?"

A Mahavakya and the mantra work together overtime. "You are not Brahman until you realize that you are Brahman" is the long and short of it. "Thou Art That" is a fact of Truth, whereas the presence of ignorance is still a problem of lingering doubt. The more one becomes convinced of the latter, the more a nondual affirmation will take one deeper. Removing an airtight wrapper from around a precious object proves the dispensability of both the wrapper and the air outside. For nondual realization, one has to go the full distance by renouncing the unreal, not just affirming the Real.

"I have been reading something in the tradition every morning before I start my meditation. What I have read and learned from you and Mother Sarasvati makes way more sense than anything I've ever known before. It has already created a clarity in my life that I've never felt. I feel like I've always been on this path and now I'm just more aware of what that means. Does this make sense?"

Sincere seekers who arrive at such auspicious times via Mother's Grace have all noted the wonder of it. Clarity, khyati, is one of Her boons upon those who are willing to learn. Now, do not deviate; this is the moment! As Ramprasad sings, "Never let the mundane opinions of the world dim the intensity of your devotion to Divine Reality in the least...."

"Sri Ramakrishna, our Lord, a simple illiterate Bengali, understood intelligence much better than our so called scholars or intellectuals, obsessed with meaningless numbers and the dark history of a war-torn and suffering world. Concerning the two boys I mentioned earlier. Sadly, they seemed to be oblivious to the greater religious history of human kind. Our discussions on religion did not reach any depth and the boys seemed to me, okay about it. They talked to me about how great numbers of people were being converted in Asia and South America. The conversion-fury of the Christian newcomers in India is of course not desirable, bringing along with them their inferior doctrines and books. On the other hand, it's nothing but wonderful to see the natural synthesis of the Indian religion. Ramakrishna's worship of non-Indian personas or elements like Jesus or Muhammed were indeed universal like the essence of India's spiritual findings.

It is very difficult to find another universal being like Sri Ramakrishna, and equally as hard to find another truly nondual philosophy like Advaita. I am not biased in this; I have just looked everywhere and cannot but help make such real and accurate comparisons like these. The Mormon philosophy is very skewed. I have even heard this from the young people of Mormon parents who came to my classes before, and who were relatives of young Vedanta students of mine. Also from the little pamphlets they pass out, which can be insulting to one's intelligence if one already knows better. The philosophy is a mess! Thus, it is possible to have strong faith in an inferior ideology, proving once again that to open up to other paths and religions is both informative and helpful in widening one's own views, and the conclusions of paths one might tread. The Four Yogas, if observed and practiced well, help us to do this naturally inside of Vedic Faith and pathways. Further, studying the life of Sri Ramakrishna Paramahamsa will reveal that to truly see Brahman/God/Allah, etc., one should look into all traditions with an open mind, but from the safe and settled position and perspective of one's own chosen religion, well-chosen and well practiced. This truth is for devotees who have already entered into spiritual life. For those who have not, or who are searching still, it is okay to look into other paths to see if one vibrates well with any given one. This is a sort of "dating period," so to speak, wherein an early aspirant will try out different perspectives. But again, there are those who merely bounce around to this path and that path, without ever finding and selecting a chosen one. These are "menu tasters," so to speak, and that tendency must be guarded against. All of the above is shared with you from my own observations and experiences as a dharma teacher here in the U.S. for nearly 50 years.

"There is a feeling that keeps coming in my mind, which is that of 'not doing enough.' I've been increasing my meditation time, increasing studying and memorization, and have been focused on progressing in karma yoga through each day, and I am constantly observing the mind's thoughts and keeping them on either the scriptures, the lives of holy beings, or the mantra, but this feeling of 'not doing enough' still persists (at times). There is the thought that 'if I just do this the feeling will go away,' but I'm thinking this is not the correct mental position. My stance as of late has been to simply ignore this and understand that this feeling will pass at some time, thus be calm. Nevertheless, I would greatly appreciate your thoughts on this 'feeling' which I recognize dwells within the non-self. It is true that every problem rests in Prakriti, and that there is no problem in the Self!"

This is the uncertain ego imposing itself on you. At least it is better than the ego-face that tells you not to do practice, yes? So use it to do more, but free of guilt and remorse, which can become great traps if you let them abide in the mind.

"I have been attempting to look at spiritual life not as something to be attained, but as something that is always present, always available for the spiritual seeker. I also have been noticing the degree of the remembrance of spiritual life. I have been reciting the Ramakrishna Chalisa daily and keeping up with my meditation, and when possible I listen to your livestreaming. It is good to be saying the mantra everyday, Sometime I count 4 rounds, sometimes I say 6, sometimes only 3. And I am observing my degree of devotion to the ideal. It seems to me that the spiritual realm is constant, it is just how our mind is that changes our perception of it. That is why keeping up Sadhana is so important. I am also becoming more aware of karma, that in this life, everything has a price to pay. One of the things that I most liked about last weekend's Satsang was how you spoke about Freedom in Advaita. I really see that this is the path for me, because in some way, the reason why I chose this path is partially because of that Freedom that Advaita preaches. I think to be a freedom-loving soul is a good quality. Two years ago, I believe we got this bookmark that showed key words of what Advaita Vedanta stands for. What would you say, or how much of a part of Advaita Vedanta is Freedom? What are the conditions of this Freedom in Advaita Vedanta, and what are its stages?"

Advaita is all about Freedom. Like what you say above about spiritual life — that it is always present — that is all the more true of Advaita Vedanta. All that you are seeking at present via sadhana, all of it forms stages that are leading you to nondual understanding. Once you have it, once you have arrived There, life will not be confusing anymore; all will be clear. All you need to do is "Go Forward."

"Are dreams about dying or formlessness a gift from higher consciousness to prepare for some kind of similar experience? A month ago I had a dream of dying of a heart attack and sank into formless blackness. It was very real, and I woke up with chest pain, and have had chest pain ever since, but doctors can't find anything. Perhaps these experiences are designed to desensitize myself to overhyping/overvaluing those kinds of experiences and merely keep an even mind regardless?"

Yes, but mainly they are for pointing out the presence of the witness of death, prior to, during, and after. You died...but you are still here. It is all dream death, because this is all dream life. Once a family man dreamed he had three fine sons. When he awoke, seeing that they were gone, he mourned them. His dream sons seemed as real to him as his living children.

"When it comes to nirvitarka samadhi, when the vrittis in the mind leading to meaning and coming in from the sense organs have ceased, and one is identifying with the knower, I have found that when one ceases the vrittis in the mind in the forms of thoughts and subtle visualizations, that there are still subtle vrittis that exist. After contemplation it seems that the ahamkara and buddhi maintain their vibration even in the absence of thoughts and visualizations in the mind. It also seems like there are subtle vrittis in the manas aspect of the antahkarana in the absence of thoughts and thought forms as well. How does one quell these residual vrittis of the various mechanisms of the fourfold mind? I immediately think that through purification and utilizing the Seven Ways of Mastering Consciousness these residual vibrations will be lessened leading to deeper meditation. I would greatly appreciate .your thoughts and advice on this. I will implement direction immediately."

The one word is constancy — one of Holy Mother's favorites. All is accomplished with its presence or, put obversely, nothing can really fructify without it. That is the conclusion of the Father of Yoga as well. He puts it in terms of the presence of very subtle samskaras, i.e., vrittis, even after the seventh limb of steady meditation has been gained. This is also true of the gunas, that they remain and re-insinuate themselves despite the aspirant's best efforts. The way I explain that is, if the soul wrought all manner of karmas for lifetimes, then an equal amount of effort in the opposite direction will need to be put forth to reverse the effects. But do not fret; you have the Great Master at your back, as also the Vedanta. One lifetime can be enough time to neutralize all karma, but not without constancy (once you have found the Guru, the sangha, and the dharma teachings).

"I have been reading the Svayambhuva Discourses from a Quintessential Yoga Vasishta recently, about the Seven Stages of True Knowledge. Contemplating certain chapters has led me to formulate a proper question. In the beginning I found that after reading so many, that they seemed too discursive, and decided not to continue them. Then I realized I should deepen the conceptual understanding. So how would you unfold Conscious Awareness as non-duality? Whether in view of ajnana bhumikas and jnana bhumikas, could we understand transcendence as an action, or an interaction per se, since the verb is so widely used in academia as well as in spiritual teachings."

Very glad to see you ruminating on Lord Vasishtha's teachings, and looking back to the grandfathers of the Solar line in India. Where else can one get good teachings on such rare things as nonduality and its meaning and facility? In answer to your question, it could be stated that nondual Reality is the only real conscious Awareness. Being only partially aware of things, as so many beings are today, is a far cry from Advaita, and may even be a contradiction in terms. How can Awareness be unawares, or Consciousness become unconscious? It never really can (and I was trying to explain that on the "Buddha at the Gas Pump" interview yesterday), but coverings can creep in and obscure It. All beings seeking Truth should be aware that they can never lose Awareness at all, because it is the only reality. Therefore, there is no need for regret, or to brood over this. Seekers must only take steps to unveil Consciousness of its coverings, or dispense with the covering power. It is much like clouds covering the sun, temporarily, or fog obscuring a valley. With this eternal fact in mind, the uncovering process will take place quickly, especially when the seeker is constantly taking up the welcome task, and thereby striving after their inherent perfection. "Unfolding" is a good word, then, and one must use it as a method toward a definite aim, rather than a hope, a fear, or an expectation.

"This recent retreat was by far the best one I've been on. I say that for a few reasons. The way you divided the classes made digesting knowledge much easier. I really appreciated the breaks between the teachings because it gave me the opportunity to wake myself up when needed, review my notes, and consider questions that might have come up before launching into the next class. I was also able to read between classes to bring more to my understanding for the next class. Also I love mauna, silence, and having it last throughout the retreat allowed me more time to be with the teachings and not get distracted with socializing. The big takeaways for me were:

Hearing that Holy Mother is an Avatar herself.

Hearing just how available Holy Mother and Sri Ramakrishna are when one is sincere. I never contemplated the concept of grace in Vedanta before and just how the Holy Mother sees us as her children. Also understanding just how the shrine functions with all the divine beings coming forth through the image when the proper attitude and sacrifice is in place.

-The other big take away was Mantra-diksha. I physically felt something move in my heart within the ceremony. I feel more serious regarding my practice and more restless/impatient when placed in worldly environments.

The practicality and simplicity of the lesson of the 5-6 P's was what I needed to hear. In particular the last P you added, Preparation, was of particular importance to me. I could have prepared way more for this retreat than I did, and then would have had more quality questions to bring to satsang. There are many aspects of my life that just flat out require more preparation."

All of this sounds like you were very aware, and very ready for such an event in your life. This is what we want, these kinds of experiences. The more of them we can have, the more the commonplace run of the mill activities we repeat monthly will lose their hold on our minds. Keep up this very good work, and remember that "Qualification is King."

"I've been contemplating the existence of Maya in terms of how does this universe of Time, Space, Causation, Name, and Form come to be. I've understood this as just like a mirage in the desert, only due to the presence and existence of the desert does the mirage exist, but one cannot say that the mirage has any true existence. Again, I've heard of Maya existing due to the 'closeness' to Brahman, and through the very proximity that it shines/exists by borrowed light. There still remains the thought that, why does this phenomenon even occur, and for what purpose if it is unreal? When I think about these questions I come to the conclusion (please correct any deluded understanding) that the very notion of 'does Maya exist or not' comes from the standpoint of ignorance and thus ones comprehension of the fact of maya is thereby deluded because it (maya) is being questioned from the standpoint of taking it as real (because the questioner is still attached to the body or mind thereby still entrapped by maya). As Shankara said, maya is inscrutable. Nevertheless, when one transcends Maya the mirage is seen for what it truly is, unreal. Thence forth, maya no longer exists and Lila is engaged in. Is my thinking about this correct? Please enlighten my thought process."

Yes, your thinking is maturing very well along the lines of this slippery slope of a subject. As you approach the nondual siddhantas, or conclusions, after your intense study period and self-inquiry is done and gels, you will feel the deeper element of finer comprehension around maya dawn in your mind. I have put it lately that higher Awareness does not see maya anymore for all has become Brahman to It. It is lower and conditioned consciousness that courts maya and its risks, and thus falls victim to its subtleties. There was a very good exchange on this topic at the class today, which is why you should learn how to work the new website and take in our new and ongoing events. Are your time restraints restricting you from doing that? Then master time!

"I would like to ask you a question that arose in my mind last night, while you were lifestreaming. Of course, AUM and Hrim are two really powerful seeds for our mantra. I'd like to ask you about the genesis of Hrim, does it "exist" via The Word, or is it a projection separate from AUM? Ideally, one should think about every mental/physical projection as something originating from the Word, but I've never heard or read about Mother being limited to the existence of the cosmic matrix/AUM. By thinking of that, could you not say that Mother is the essence of both AUM and Hrim?"

Hrim (Hring) is Mother's own bijam, along with a few other all-powerful seed words. AUM, they say, is the essential word of Brahman. Put the two together and you have keys for form, and the key for Formlessness, which when put with the name of the Kali Avatar, becomes the most effective and current Mahamantra for the age. We never talk about Brahman and Shakti as being separate, but always united, like fire and its power to burn. "They appear as two, are ever one, and give rise to the many." With Divine Mother, She is supremely Self-willed, thus is Divine Reality in Its dynamic phase. That is why Sri Ramakrishna said, pointing to His wife, Sarada, "She is my power; without Her I cannot even lift my finger." Divine Mother is not a "mental/physical projection" of our minds, or any mind. Rather, all minds originate in Her. Thus, She is the Source of everything. When thought of simultaneously with Brahman, She is the Divine Matrix via which the Formless, Actionless, Causeless Being is able to express Itself. Otherwise It would remain ever and always amorphous, homogenous, and boundless, which It does anyway, despite being seemingly pressed into form.

"I intended to ask you this question during satsang yesterday but was not persistent enough. Also this is a question about the yamas/morality, so I was not sure if it would fit within the spiritual framework; I also was not sure if it was too personal a question. Here is the question: How can I practice satya with someone who is defensive and sensitive? My daily interactions with my biological mother inspired this question, however I think the better question is, how can I apply this to myself because I recognize within me a sensitivity and defensiveness too which can get in the way of my growth? I keep thinking of Swamiji saying that he wants a man-making philosophy, a philosophy that emphasizes strength. I want more strength in my life and think that for me this needs to start with truth, honesty, and straightforwardness within myself. Do you have any thoughts, suggestions, and or practices for me in this sphere?"

Basically, the yama of satya is both difficult to attain, and to maintain in daily life as well. As the story goes.....

The young Kauravas and Pandavas were learning their first lessons. The acharya pronounced the Vedic text: Satyam vada, dharmam chara, "Speak the truth, follow the path of righteousness," and asked the pupils to repeat. Everyone then repeated it. The teacher asked them to memorize the text. The next day he asked what they had learnt the previous day. All pronounced: "satyam vada, dharmam chara," except Yudhishthira. Surprised, the acharya asked why couldn't he, the eldest and the brightest among the one hundred and five pupils, learn such a simple lesson? What Yudhishthira said in reply was an indication of his future greatness as the exemplar par-excellence of truth. He plainly confessed that he had not yet learnt to speak the truth. Others might have memorized the few words, but that certainly was not the purport of this short but profound precept: satyam vada — speak the truth. Unless one speaks the truth in day-to-day life, what use was it to merely memorize a few words? It took years of relentless practice and untold suffering for Yudhishthira to practice this precept in life — to truly learn that kindergarten lesson.

Regarding defensiveness, it is common inside of families, and hard to get rid of, too. With a combination of compassion for the others mixed with abiding forbearance and careful nonreactivity, one can improve. These are a worthwhile addition to one's character, to be sure.

"In your commentary in lesson #28 of Raja Yoga you describe something which seems to be very similar if not the same as the Dissolution of the Mindstream meditation. It is mentioned that one makes a conscious offering and dissolution of the gross and subtle elements, the gross and subtle objects, the universe, the ten senses, the three-fold mind, and the ego into oneness. My mind is thinking that by following that meditation one will have to merge the perceiver, the perceived, and the process of perceiving into one state of oneness. Additionally, through this inward journey, any impediments in the mind that are attached/correlated with those tattvas will come up and must be rendered neutral (for instance by focusing and internalizing the Immutables of the Paramatman and the 13 inherent characteristics of Atman) with the power of one's own concentration in order to quell the vrittis associated with the particular tattva and dissolve it/return it to its cause (that the particular tattva is the effect of). It seems that through this process, one will:
*Work a groove in the mind leading to the Self that will become easier to follow in time and with effort;
*Be able to focus on the Perceiver aspect of the process, thus gaining the knowledge of that ever present Presence, as well as knowing that all this 'motion of dissolution' is really occurring in Truth, and is one with It (if the meditation is successfully completed);
*Be able to hone in on the instrument of perception/dissolution as well as the objects/view that is being perceived. Is this thinking correct?"

Not only is this correct thinking, it is deep thinking with good conclusions. My only comment is, that the groove you mention above is the replacing of samskaras with potential samskaras of samadhi, which Patanjali brings into the sutras at a later time. Otherwise, there are those grooves most beings create back to the world of more suffering. Aspirants must "fill those in," then drive new ones in, and deeper.

Further, the dissolution of the mindstream is really present in many forms throughout all of India's darshanas. The advantage in the Sankhya and Yoga darshanas is that we get to use the 24 Tattvas, and further, that dharma teachers caan move to bring out insights like hidden impurities attached to the various tattvas, changing the whole focus onto not just cosmology, but also, and importantly, to sadhana. Truth realized via practice far outstrips reading and study alone, which when meditation is added in, mellows even further.

"Are all pathways and spiritual teachers acceptable ways leading to Brahman?"

If they are truly spiritual in nature, then yes. But to be spiritual is to be based in a profoundly realized philosophy, brought to earth via the contemplations and meditations of illumined souls. Also, such authentic pathways need to be sweetened in the syrup of bhakti, love for the Lord. A final sign of their authenticity will be that they encourage both nonviolence and selfless service of God in mankind. On the other hand, signs of false paths and prophets show up in a so-called religion's usage of domination and war to enslave and convert other races and nations, and their enjoyment of ill-gotten gains extracted from cultures that they disrespected by their evil and selfish actions. To quote Swami Vivekananda, for example: "Preachers that come over here from Christian lands have that one antiquated foolishness of an argument that because the Christians are powerful and rich and the Hindus are not, so Christianity must be better than Hinduism. To which the Hindus aptly retort that that is the very reason why Hinduism is a religion and Christianity is not; because in this beastly world it is blackguardism and that alone which prospers, and virtue always suffers."

Religion should never be mixed with politics; that is a mistake. Realized souls, when they are left alone to meditate, come forth later as the only real world teachers. Then, they can be referred to as counsel by the ruling classes in society. Meditation makes them simultaneously universally-minded and compassionate, while members/leaders of the priest class who seek money and support from politicians and rulers become involved in war in the name of religion, turning it into irreligion.

"How is it that when this body was birthed fresh from subtler realms, I had no recollection at all of even the slightest sliver of that?"

There are two main reasons: first, if you came from the ancestors via lower heaven when you took rebirth, you (your mental complex) had to pass through the densest part of the "curtain of nescience" to get to earth, which stripped you of all memories from before. You emerged from your mother's womb (be careful how you choose parents!) as if with a clean (mental) slate, with no memories. But there were deeper ones (samskaras) lurking. Those got covered and had no time to rise up in you due to the society routing you immediately towards a money-making education, instead of teaching you to be still and silent via meditation, and taking in the dharma.

Secondly, your part in this vicious cycle (that ends in death in ignorance and rebirth to do it all over again), is that you would not wake up when opportunities came, i.e., when God came calling. To your credit you found a path and teacher early on due to good karma. But as you know, it takes more than good karma to snap the chains of rebirth in ignorance, for you have seen how even good people suffer here, and seldom reach The Goal. It needs follow-through and perseverance. Then only, with the help of great souls, will you quit making primal errors, quit wasting time with pleasures, quit forming more karmas, good and bad, that keep you in the samsaric cycle of rebirth.

This is a long answer, but there is much more to it. Once you know such answers, the time is upon you to practice using the tools that have been given to you by the knower of all answers. That is why the Holy Mother said, "We (the lovers of God), have not come here to have fun; we know how precious this birth is." Do you see the fun-seekers out there, and their folly? They are, to quote one source I heard from early on in my life, the "God-damned pleasure-lovers." Do not go down their path.

"When it comes to transcending the 'ideas of objects' does this mean that one is transcending the vrittis in the mind that objects (and the sounds thereof) have a tendency to create (due to the uncontrolled mind)? Or is this more along the lines of reaching a state of mind that is beyond the conception of objects (meaning there is no subtle object (i.e. a thought) in the mind for perception)?"

Transcendence is an unmistakable word. Simply forgoing the objects is a start, but higher samadhis can enter if one ends the train of thoughts around and about them. If one does not strike a tuning fork, it remains silent. The same is true of the mind. Allow it to remain quiet, unstruck, like The Word. "Objectless" Reality will be the result, peaceful and transcendent.

"Is it true that the intention to spread one's personal way of thinking by force is an occult power? What is that called, and how is it avoided."

Not only individuals, but whole classes of individuals fall victim to this evil tendency. A nation, over all, including its religion, can and often does run along that wayward tract. Hinduism, Buddhism, and Jainism are exceptions to that temptation, though the former has fallen into it of late, to some extent. It is the occult power of anima that we speak of here. It is the first of the eight, and the other seven can be clearly seen as relating to it. That is, the power of domination (ishitva) via war is further inflamed by covetousness (laghima), meddlesomeness due to jealousy (prapti), materialism (prakamya), attempts towards mastering and manipulating (like splitting atoms) nature (mahima), curiosity about psychic phenomena (lagima), the over-riding desire to enjoy pleasure (vashitva), and seeking mastery over others by vainly influencing them to enjoy wealth and pleasure (kama-vasayita). In this endeavor, the West, with its champion of America, is proceeding. In fostering peace (ahimsa) and harmony/unity, the East, with its champion of India, is striving for notice.

"Beings like Lord Buddha and Sri Ramakrishna have pointed out that too much cleverness is a danger to spiritual advancement, and even breeds more attachment to the world through egotism. It seems that the present day provides a lot of room for such egos to grow and come to power. There are smart people out there, no doubt, but so many of them are taking advantage of others to better their own prospects. Why is this happening, and what can stop it?"

Qualities such as selflessness, compassion for others, service of God in mankind, are the solutions. The method is to go after such attributes and attain them, though everything in the world is against such progress. So, one gives up the world. That act often lifts the soul up and out of the world, and to a "better place," as is said. Therefore, of the few souls who succeed in renouncing life in the world, only a small percentage of them will develop the strong will and desire to return to earth and keep working for its betterment. These few will have to contend with the stodginess of matter, the overall unwillingness of the masses, the averse will of the ancestors who want to continue the cycle, the threatening presence of deluded minds that favor war and violence, and the workings of maya itself that naturally covers and distorts pathways leading to real progress.

Amidst all this resistance live those clever souls who see all that takes place in mind and maya as an opportunity to increase their enjoyment and amass possessions, even at the cost of the suffering of others. They will not pay heed if you tell them, "What will it avail a man to gain a kingdom but lose his soul?" They do not think or act from the soul, but from the imbalanced mind. They do not know that if you help another being, that will help you, and if you harm others, that harm will return to you. And this may well be the answer to the question people ask regarding why there is loss and suffering. Only harsh lessons will get through to gross and insensitive minds — those clever ones whom you ask about here. Unfortunately, collateral damage, as they call it, will also take place.

"Thank you for helping me with a spiritual touch. I am happy to say that I no longer have those jealousy issues to the same extent as I did back then. However, defensiveness is a thing for me at times and I feel that it could be sprouting from a subtler sense of jealousy still. I was just reading from Voice of Freedom where Swamiji said 'Jealousy is a terrible, horrible sin. It enters a man so mysteriously.' This really stood out to me and I want to root jealousy out. Would acts of service be a good method to combat any subtle and/or gross occurrences of jealousy?"

Yes, very good; you have all the right intentions. Do selfless service, without reaction to obstacles and feelings, as often as you can, and that will go a long way towards rooting out subtle tendrils of jealousy. The aspirant must extend efforts over a period of time, and not just rely upon what company with the guru and good cycles of gunas offer. Old habits which one thought to be gone might return otherwise.

"I walked away from class today with a lot of sublime material to contemplate. I practice the method of meditation that you prescribed me at my time of initiation, and I hardly deviate from that. However, I almost feel like my mind is rebelling against me as of late, like it wants to do something different? I was going to try meditating on a few of the things that you mentioned in class today, such as the space beyond stillness, or thinking of oneself to be the sun, casting its rays on everything. However, I've also learned that when my meditations become a bit dry, what helps is to take up a book on Ma Sarada, to rejuvenate my bhakti. I can see the benefit of sticking with a singular approach in meditation, so that the mind's cycles are easier to watch. However, I would treasure any advice you have to give on this front."

I feel that you are advanced enough, and have enough meditation time under your belt, that you could mix in a few of these other practices. Do not deviate from the original instructions, overall, but be a little spontaneous when you feel the call. Even if you have success in a few of these experimental meditation techniques, always go back to the root one, and you will be fine.

And importantly, let me know the outcome of such experiments, so I can guide and give input.

"Can you give me an example of a spiritual aspirant transcending the apparent and piercing through the subtle to arrive at the final renunciation?"

I can do better than that. Penetrate through what is before you, like science has seen through solid objects to find particles. But do not stop there. Introduce yourself to the billions of particles of your own thoughts via conscious contemplation and meditation. Split them with your mind's eye to release living intelligence. Renunciation of appearances will then become easier, and will turn natural. Bliss will occur, and the soul will saturate itself more and more in that ocean — like a salt doll diving in to try and measure its depths. Do not worry about giving up things up. As Swamiji states, "Do not try to give up things in nature; they will give you up." So try instead to give up delusions in the mind. When they are gone, and with the mind working perfectly, Nature will become tiresome to you, and will drop away naturally. As Sri Ramakrishna put it, "Then you will seek the gardener, and not the garden...."

"When Swamiji states that the Prana exists in an 'almost motionless state' before a cycle begins, is the correct understanding of this that the only pure motionless 'state' is Brahman/Atman, thus all attributes, even in their unmanifested state, have a vibration? Thus true Pranayama is not just controlling the breath, but also the ability of the aspirant to withdraw the Prana to its unmanifested state; is this correct? Would this be similar to Sasmita Samadhi, where the vrittis of the mind have been quelled to such an extent that only the Ahamkara is subtly vibrating? Meaning if the Prana is in an almost motionless state, there is a subtle sense of 'I' that is present? Am I on the right thought process?"

Yes, and very good. The "potential" for vibration rests in seeds held by the unmanifested state. These seeds have already been "watered" and have thereby sprouted in the manifested state. Beyond both, says Sri Krishna, once again, there is the Supremely Unmanifested State. That, the Brahman State, is truly nonvibrational in essence.

The seeker tries to go beyond even The Word in meditation, as well as beyond the Trinity that utilizes It to project worlds in space and time. All mediums and matrixes for Consciousness, then, no matter how high, will have to "get thee behind me," in order that Awareness in its original Essence be revealed, and mankind finally come to know the true Self, Atman, is vibrationless.

Questions regarding problems in spiritual life may be directed to Nectar's editorial staff at: srvinfo@srv.org

◆ *Rabbi Rami Shapiro*

SHMITA
A Year of Releasing

Judaism is not a world religion. That is to say Judaism has no interest in converting the world to its way of thinking and acting. If not for the exile of the Jews from their homeland and the appropriation of Judaism by Christianity (which is a world-conquering religion), few people would know about Judaism at all. Yet even with exile and appropriation Jewish practice is largely limited to those few millions who identify as Jews.

Years ago my rebbe (guru) Reb Zalman Schachter-Shalomi charged me with bringing my understanding of Judaism to the world beyond Jews the way so many Hindu and Buddhist teachers have brought their traditions to the world. This essay is part of that effort.

My focus in this essay is the practice of shmita/releasing. What I offer isn't a strictly Jewish read of shmita, but a universal application of shmita that draws from but stretches beyond Judaism.

My goal here is not simply to teach about shmita but to help you engage with the practice of shmita as you read the essay. I do this through a series of questions I invite you to answer as you read. Please make time to engage with the questions as I ask them.

Shmita an Introduction

Every seven years Judaism calls us to a year-long act of economic, social, and spiritual revolution called Shmita, a year of releasing. This year, 5782 in the Jewish calendar, is one of those years. We first learn about Shmita in the Book of Exodus:

"For six years you may sow your land and gather in its produce, but in the seventh year you are to let the land go (shm'tenah) and to let it be (nitashta), that the needy may eat of what grows of its own accord, and that the wildlife may eat of what the needy leave behind. Do this not only with your fields, but with your vineyards and olive groves as well." (Exodus 23:10-11)

A few more details are added in the Book of Leviticus:

"Six years you shall sow your field, and six years you shall prune your vineyard, and gather in their yield; but in the seventh year there shall be a sabbath of complete rest for the land, a sabbath for YHVH: you shall not sow your field or prune your vineyard. You shall not reap what grows of your unsown fields or gather the grapes of your unpruned vine: it shall be a year of complete rest for the land. You may eat what the land produces of its own accord — you, your servants and laborers, your livestock and the wild animals — all may eat freely of what the land produces of its own accord." (Leviticus 25:3-7)

The Personal Dimension of Shmita

While the origins of Shmita rest in an ancient agrarian civilization, its value is no less profound when understood in light of our own time. This becomes clear when we challenge ourselves to engage with the idea fo Shmita in our personal lives. To this end we focus our attention on Shmita's three foundational ideas: shm'tenah (let it go), nitashta (let it be) and Shabbat la YHVH (a Sabbath for YHVH).

Shm'tenah (let it go) & Nitashta (let it be)

The difference between shm'tenah (let it go) and nitashta (let it be) is this: to let something go is to free yourself from that something; to let something be is to allow that something to be what it is free from your efforts to make of it conform to what you want it to be.

Take a few moments and think about and answer the following questions.

* What do I need to let go of in myself; what ideas, dreams, hopes, assumptions, beliefs, stories, etc. need releasing?

* How might my life change if I did in fact release these things?

* What people do I need to let go of in my life?

*How might my life change if I did let these people go?

* How might the lives of these people change if I did in fact let them go?

* What do I need to let be in myself?

What might happen if I did let these things be?

Shabbat la YHVH

The third foundational idea of Shmita is Shabbat la YHVH (Leviticus 25:4). YHVH, the central name of God in Judaism, comes from the Hebrew verb "to be". YHVH is a verb rather than a noun and is best understood as Being: not a being or even a Supreme Being but the process of being itself that manifests as the universe and everything in it. YHVH is the beingness of all beings or the happening of all happening, what the 18th century rabbi Menachem Nachum Twersky called Chiut, Aliveness.

Comprised as it is of four consonants and no vowels, the

name YHVH is literally ineffable. To avoid the awkwardness of trying to pronounce a word that cannot be pronounced, the ancient rabbis substituted Adonai (Lord) for YHVH, reducing God to a masculine noun supporting a patriarchal hierarchy. Sticking with the original Hebrew Shabbat la YHVH rather than its rabbinic substitute Shabbat ladonai Shmita is a year devoted to being rather than becoming, to being rather than having.

The psychologist Erich Fromm tells us that having and being are "two fundamental modes of existence, two different kinds of orientation toward self and the world:

"In the having mode of existence my relation to the world is one of possessing and owning, one in which I want to make everybody and everything, including myself, my property. In the being mode of existence [we are talking about] aliveness and authentic relatedness to the world...the true nature, the true reality, of a person or a thing in contrast to deceptive appearances...." (Erich Fromm *To Have or To Be*, p. 24)

In the having mode you are separate from and even alien to the world around you, and your very survival depends on dominating that world and bending it to your will. In the being mode of existence you realize that there is no "other," no separation between you and the world. Everything goes with everything else, and your survival (as well as your happiness) depends on working with the world rather than against it.

Working with the world is like swimming with the current rather than against it, or cutting wood with the grain rather than across it. This is what the Chinese Taoists call wei wu wei: non-coercive action. Wei wu wei arises naturally when you are aware of the way things are at any given moment, and act harmoniously with them.

Shabbat la YHVH is a period of time in which we practice non coercive action and drop the habit of having and adopt the habit of being. The question you must ask yourself regarding this is How? To help you move deeply into this question, we suggest you first tackle a few preliminary questions:

* How is my life devoted to having?
* What moments can I recall that were in tune with being?
* What actions might I put aside this year to shift my life from having to being?
* What new actions might I adopt this year to shift my life from having to being?
* What benefits might I derive from making this shift?
* How might friends and loved ones assist me in making this shift?
* How might friends and loved one resist my making this shift?
* What is one thing I can do in the next day or two to begin the process of Shmita and shifting my life from having to being during the next twelve months?

Sadly, shmita is a Jewish practice few Jews take seriously. By focusing on the agricultural nature of the practice in the ancient Land of Israel, they relegate the practice to farmers living in Israel and avoid the challenge of releasing and letting be shmita places before them. In this short essay I have taken shmita out of its ancient setting and presented it as a practice for the world. While there is much more that can be done with shmita especially in the context of environmental justice and climate change, it is my hope that you will find in shmita a challenge you can adapt to your own life regardless of your religion or even lack thereof. We can all benefit from a year of releasing and letting be.

> "Working with the world is like swimming with the current rather than against it, or cutting wood with the grain rather than across it. This is what the Chinese Taoists call wei wu wei: non-coercive action. Wei wu wei arises naturally when you are aware of the way things are at any given moment, and act harmoniously with them."

Rabbi Rami Shapiro is an award-winning author, poet, essayist, and educator whose poems have been anthologized in over a dozen volumes, and whose prayers are used in prayer books around the world. Rami received rabbinical ordination from the Hebrew Union College–Jewish Institute of Religion and holds doctoral degrees in both Jewish studies and divinity. A congregational rabbi for 20 years, Rabbi Shapiro currently teaches Religious Studies at Middle Tennessee State University, and directs One River (www.one-river.org), a not-for-profit educational foundation devoted to building community through contemplative conversation. Rami writes a regular column for Spirituality and Health Magazine called Roadside Assistance on Your Spiritual Journey. His most recent books are The Sacred Art of Lovingkindness, The Divine Feminine, and Open Secrets from which this essay was adapted. Rabbi Rami can be reached through his website, www.rabbirami.com

◆ *Babaji Bob Kindler*

SRI RAMAKRISHNA'S NEW DISPENSATION & SWAMI VIVEKANANDA'S NEO-VEDANTA

Fresh Wisdom Transmission & Conclusively Matured Nonduality

With the surprising advent on the world scene of Sri Ramakrishna and Swami Vivekananda, a host of new avenues have opened up for spiritual aspirants to take advantage of. There need be no more fear of making the ages-old mistake of following questionable gurus and charlatans, in any religion, for the obvious Light of this dynamic duo has penetrated those dark quarters, dispersing ignorance and awakening sleeping souls to their inner potential. And if the question be asked why the world is still in its usual turmoil and confusion after such an advent, the answer is simple. The world will always be in such a state, and always has been in such a turmoil. That will not change, ever. It is those rare and few sincere, seeking souls that know the earth is a hole in the ground and that life here is only a momentary sojourn, who leave the world of matter to its own devices and turn to extract the essence of wisdom from the Great Souls who arrive here. For, as Sri Krishna has stated so long ago, knowledge is the best of all purifiers.

Sri Ramakrishna's incomparable spiritual abilities were bestowed upon the entire world in one visitation. He blew out the birthday candles of billions of souls with one breath. Now – and even though some 5 or 6 million beings have begun to get the idea of the birthlessness and deathlessness of their Souls (*Atman*) – billions more must follow. He, Himself, said that He would remain in the subtle body, close to earth, for some three hundred years after His ascension, so that seeking souls could penetrate the world-bewitching maya and attain salvation and liberation. To understand this, and more of what He brought forth for us, the chart included with this article, on the facing page, can be scrutinized.

Five-Fold New Dispensation

Under the five-fold list of the facets of Sri Ramakrishna's descent on the chart, the fifth one has just been mentioned. Penetrating the world-bewitching maya is no easy feat, not just because it is dense and all-attracting, but because it is also so subtle that most beings do not perceive it. It is like the air one breathes but which one does not see, and which gets taken for granted in the interim. If a man could come amongst a community of forest dwellers who had never even seen a trail, and convince them of a path through the woods lying nearby, that would describe to some extent what Sri Ramakrishna did when He came to earth in 1836. Even India, usually so radiant with spiritual light, was facing a deep dive into despondency and delusion, brought about by a weakening of its inner fabric due to the decline of the priest class and the resultant evils of their ritualistic craft. This allowed other evils, such as the English invasion into the country, to transpire. And this wanton intrusion by Western nations saw them entering into a phase of increased wealth and power, and the power of domination that accompanies them. They were foolishly drinking the wine of power straight from the cup of *maya*, and creating suffering and *karmas* untold for themselves, and for the world. As Swami Vivekananda explains this dichotomy: *"Every new thought must create opposition – in the civilized a polite sneer, in the vulgar savage, howls and filthy scandal. Even these earthworms must stand erect, even children must see the light. The Americans are drunk with new wine. But a hundred waves of prosperity have come and gone over my country. We have learned the lesson which no child can understand: It is vanity, this hideous world is maya."*

The fact that Sri Ramakrishna was on the scene in India during the latter period of England's occupation was a divine dictate designed to protect the core of Indian spirituality, despite what occurred with the colonization of the Hindu people and the robbery of India's resources thereafter. All the nefarious doings and goings-on perpetrated by nations upon other nations fits the title of *maya* quite adequately. When a Great Soul, an *Avatar*, for instance, visits the earth realm, the darkness of *maya* in the form of insentient nature, as well as the ignorance of living beings under the mantle of deluded mind, vanishes. Truth, being the *"most corrosive substance in the three worlds,"* as Vivekananda said it, burns through such coverings in no time, though it takes longer where such dense obscuration is the thickest. The mere presence of a Great Light such as Sri Ramakrishna acts to strip superimpositions away and reveal openings that were previously hidden by the darkness of ages. He is like the explorer with a torch who suddenly enters a cave that has been dark for thousands of years, dispelling that gloom as He moves about the cave. More on this facet of the New Dispensation will be revealed as the other four main aspects (there are, of course. additional minor aspects to His descent) are "explored."

The effect of the Great Master's appearance amidst collective consciousness has been stated, above. His unique way uncovers more of the secret of Divine Descent which is shown to humanity every so many centuries, and ages. Since embodied beings here on earth, and in heaven with the ancestors, do not remember their lifetimes due to lack of cultivating their higher awareness while in the body on earth, recollection of the *Avatar's* coming and going is generally forgotten by them in each lifetime. Yes, religious history proclaims the appearance of such singular souls, but such telling does not go that far in convincing beings who are under the illusion of *maya* of the truth of this unique phenomenon, so it becomes a matter of belief and faith. But belief suffers horribly

Sri Ramakrishna's New Dispensation & Swami Vivekananda's Neo-Vedanta

"All great Personalities should be duly honored, but homage should be paid now to the Great Master. The previous Incarnations were all right, but they have been synthesized in the person of Ramakrishna. In point of character, Paramahamsa Deva beats all previous record, and as regards teaching He was more liberal, more original, and more progressive than all of His predecessors." — Swami Vivekananda

Brought Divine Mother Reality to Earth
Awakened Truth-Seekers to the Possibility of Samadhi
Proclaimed and Proved the Validity of all World Religions
Revealed the Secret Way of The Avatar in Modern Times
Showed Humanity the Spiritual Path out of Maya

Shed New Light on the Timeless Truth of Advaita
Unveiled and Commended the Avatar of the Age to all Beings
Brought Back India's Eternal Religion of the Four Yogas
Delivered India's Incomparable Spirituality to the World
Revealed Mankind's Nature to be Perfect, not Sinful

"One day, as Narendra was laughing with a friend at the absurd notion that everything was Brahman, the Master came out from his room and touched him. Suddenly spellbound, he perceived that everything in the world was indeed God — cabs, horses, streams of people. Returning home in a dazed state, he found there, too, that food, plates, the eater, the people around him, were all God. He could hardly go about his day! When after a few days the experience abated a little, he realized that the words of the Vedanta were true."
The Gospel of Sri Ramakrishna

ADVAITA-SATYAM-AMRITAM   13

under the regime of human convention, and how can faith get developed when it was either compromised by the shaking of belief, or not there in the first place at the beginning of any given lifetime? Even beings who live at the time of the descent of such special Souls have a hard time believing in Them, what to speak of those who live later and have to look back through the eyes of religion to get a glimpse.

For those who are born with faith, however, as well as those who are on fire with the yearning to know what is beyond birth and death in the human form, the *Avatar* is the beacon for the Light of the Eternal Truth. The atmosphere that is palpable when souls are with Him/Her, as well as what He/She leaves behind after Their passing, is this New Dispensation, for those with eyes to see, lights their path through many lifetimes to the Ultimate Goal, what Lord Buddha called the *Paragatam*. For, just like everything else in the realm of name and form in time and space (*maya*), the *Avatar* also returns. As a bloodhound does not forget the scent it was given by its master, souls who seek Truth over time will never forget the past appearances of this One Divinity who takes various forms throughout phases of existence. His/Her visage is impressed, indelibly, upon their mind's consciousness. Even the changing of the outer appearance, and the shifting of religions accomplished by the *Avatar*, will not throw them off the scent, or the trail. This path of the *Ishvara* Form, called *Avataravada* in India, has its devout adherents, and they keep the path fresh and open for sincere souls.

A third aspect of the New Dispensation of Sri Ramakrishna Paramahamsa has to do with this shifting from religion to religion just mentioned. It is often noted by the *rishis* of India in their scriptures that there are three divisions of devotees: one that is conventional and tied into one religion only; another that is free from restricting conventions and open to Truth in whatever form it comes their way; and a third who is of a universal nature and mind and fully aware that the *Avatar* is both the Refuge of all conscious beings and the Home of all religious traditions. From the ranks of this third subdivision spring knowers of *dharma* and realizers of Truth — they who are called *Ishvarakotis* in the Vedic tradition. They accompany the *Avatar* to earth from age to age, and it is from them that beings receive vibrations of Intelligent Light in the form of liberating teachings. They are likened to the huge waves that take shape in the ocean after a steam-liner passes by. Though they are not restricted to any specific religion, they will be born among or come to them for the purpose of spreading the current *Avatar's* fresh message to others, regardless of their religious preferences.

Universality, and Careless Affirmation of It

In Sri Ramakrishna's unique case — He being the representative of God present in this dark age called the *Kali Yuga* — it is said that no one previous to Him had ever proven the inseparable identity of all religious traditions with one another, though some had spoken of it. Importantly, He did not state that all religions were "the same," as some have tried to explain it, but that their essence was the same. As the *Rig Veda* put it, in most ancient times, beings get to the mountaintop via various paths through the forest (of maya). The methods used by practitioners of various religions, for instance, can vary, but even here one can see, via even a cursory observance, that many of these practices are verisimilar, i.e., that devotions, study of scriptures, meditation, prayer, selfless service, etc., remain fundamental to attaining love of God and the seeking after Truth.

> "It is often noted by the rishis of India in their scriptures that there are three divisions of devotees: one that is conventional and tied into one religion only; another that is free from restricting conventions and open to Truth in whatever form it comes their way; and a third who is of a universal nature and mind and fully aware that the Avatar is both the Refuge of all conscious beings and the Home of all religious traditions."

Though much can be written and said about the unity of all religions, and the Universalism that this *Avatar* brought forward for the world to consider, a cautionary measure must be added into the mix. It concerns the fact that the *Avatar* is immersed in the Bliss of God, thus also, the state of Nonduality (*advaita*). This is an unimaginable condition to most beings on "planet" earth (the earth and all planets actually exist in the Great Mind, not in Nature, for Nature, itself, originates from the mind). The point of bringing this up as a caution, is that there will always be personages who misinterpret the *Avatar* and His salient works (like the church fathers did with Jesus's message), imaging that He/She was born on earth to prove Truth via relative activities. The truth is that He/She, existing always in Bliss and Wisdom, is intensely searching for God everywhere, and since That/It/God/Brahman is veiled here amidst matter and materialism, must venture forth and remove the coverings which impede Its vision. They do this for the sake of Love, not for the sake of proof. Thus, when Sri Sarada Devi heard that people at the collegiate and intellectual level were all excited about a man who appeared who proved the equality of all religions, She said that She never saw Him doing that; rather, that He searched the content of every religious tradition because He loved God alone, and wanted to experience God through every avenue.

Another important element of this aspect of the New Dispensation of Sri Ramakrishna, is the way such a being goes about exemplifying Truth in front of others. When excitable but naïve beings hear of the unity of all religions, and due, in part, to their aversion to performing any intense practice to achieve such a high aim, they immediately assume that they can be universalists like Him, as if with the snap of a finger. But the Great Master revealed, Himself, that in order to love and know all religions, one had to practice them all, and had to do so to the exclusion of all but the one being focused upon at any given time. Thus, He took out all images of His beloved Mother Kali from His room when He practiced the Muslim religion, and even took His food in the Muslim quarter of the temple during that phase of practice. He was rewarded for this with a vision of Mohammed. The story He told about this unique mode of practice was that of cows let loose into the pasture in the morning to graze amongst each other indiscriminately, but at dusk, the farmer brought them all back into the barn, and each was given its own stall for the milking process.

Thus, beings do have their own religious Ideal in their hearts, and should adhere to that. But seeing the problems of hypocrisy that grow among the fundamentalists of religion on earth — like misunderstandings among cultures and races, the decline of one religion and the rise of another simultaneously, the death of philosophy due to one-sided faith, and war due to religious narrowness, to name a few — an arms-open policy is wisest and best. One can hold onto the pole of their own, select tradition, then, and whirl around on it with open eyes that see all the beauty of other traditions around them. Such is the lesson, or lessons, in the New Dispensation of Sri Ramakrishna.

The penultimate principle of these five facets of Sri Ramakrishna's New Dispensation concerns a stateless state, a conditionless condition, called by the word *samadhi* in Sanskrit. It is the natural state of the pure mind, its nondual essence. Mother India has really been the one country that has given birth to a cross-section of illumined souls who attained this state, then left instructions behind on its attainment. This "attainment" is really a deep remembrance, as India's *rishis* and luminaries revealed. In Sri Ramakrishna's case, the kinds of *samadhis* He experienced staggers the imagination, as does the number of times He went into them. India's copious scriptures, as well as the *Brahmin* priests who memorized and studied them, could not account for many of these. It was as if the Great Master was bringing back long-forgotten states of illumined mind not experienced since ancient times, and living in them out in front of desire-bound materialistic modern man. For those beings who lived near to Him, like His apostles, this was a great boon, and for seekers along the path of spirituality it acted as an impetus for them to exert more intensely in order to open the mind to the blessing of such rarefied experiences.

According to *Patanjala Yoga*, the kinds of *samadhi* really amount to two, one formless (*nirupa*) and the other with form (*sarupa*). The first kind is free of qualities (*nirguna*), while the second takes them on (*saguna*). Thus, the first kind contains no seeds for further manifestation (*nirbija, i.e., asamprajnata*), while the second still has them in potential for germination (*sabija, i.e., samprajnata*). Again, the first is devoid of the mind's projections in space and time (*nirvikalpa*), while the second is open to expression therein (*savikalpa*). Finally, the first is singular, meaning there is only one of It. The second kind is multiple, as the Father of Yoga, Patanjali, so nicely describes in his *Yoga Sutras*. With this little crash course in the outer meaning of *samadhi* given out, the fifth principle of The Great Master's New Dispensation can be explored.

The most important facet of this New Dispensation under scrutiny is the unveiling of the otherwise and usually hidden presence of the Divine Mother of the Universe, called *Mahashakti*, or *Mahamaya*, by the seers. It was Sri Ramakrishna's special task to bring Her into the human context on this earth (*Bhurloka*), at this time (*Kali Yuga*). Her lack of obvious and forward presence over cycles of time on earth leaves the planet and its people devoid of protection. This outer level void is only made worse by the lack of Wisdom on the internal level, wherein beings lacking any real intelligence begin to wreak violence on the world, and even religion declines faster. Only those dedicated to Her, always and ever, afford themselves of both protection and higher knowledge, no matter what the age. The *Upanisads* state this as well, by saying: "*Following the path of Yoga, the ancient rishis of India espied the devatmashakti who, though always veiled by Her own modes of nature (the gunas), nevertheless is always present and indivisible, and who had been veiled to their awareness earlier due to the limitations of their own intellects.*" Knowing Her once, they establish themselves in Her for all time or, as the poet-saint, Ramprasad puts it: "*Once catching a glimpse of Her incomparable beauty, no other forms can they enjoy.*"

By loving Mother Kali first and foremost, Sri Ramakrishna opened the gate for Her entrance onto the world scene, and at a time that it was most needed. One devotional song to Him sings:

"O great teacher, illumined yogi, devotee of the Divine Mother and Avatar of the age. O supreme soul of my soul, accept my prostrations, accept my salutations.

You have awakened Mother Kali, the destroyer of evil, from the sacred cremation grounds of India, and with the nectar of Her Holy Name, you have flooded the land once again.
Your mighty austerities have brought the presence of the golden age into this age of ignorance and sent the healing waters of India's sacred places to all peoples and all countries around the world.

In Temple, Mosque, and Church, You worshipped God with equal reverence. Now your blessed Name is worshipped throughout the three worlds. O Supreme Leader of our souls, accept our prostrations, accept our eternal salutations."

Mother Kali is associated with cremation grounds in India because 1. She reveals to beings that their Soul (*Atman*) is birthless and deathless, and 2. She affirms for them that they are not the body. Further, She shows beings that the worlds within (*lokas/akashas*) are dreamlike places of transition and transmigration, and that *Brahman* is beyond all these. And so, looking back on Sri Ramakrishna's *samadhis*, which showed Him both the inner worlds and the realmless Realm of transcendence, the real meaning of Their divine relationship comes clear. This Presence of Divinity on the earth amidst benighted people must be counted as precious. It also needs tending here, as the Neo-Vedanta of Swami Vivekananda, to be explored next, will demonstrate.

> "Truth, in India, has been considered timeless, thus eternal in all cycles of time (mahayugas), no matter how many times they get repeated. Some opine that truth in the form of scripture simply recurs throughout history. Others insist that it comes from the finest intellects of mankind. Others propose that it comes from the highest aspect of God in Form, namely Ishvara/Ishvari. But the illumined seers of India conclude that it does not come and go at all, but is ever present; it even exists in seed form at the end of a long cycle of manifestation."

Swami Vivekananda's Neo-Vedanta: His Advaitic Reformation

The term, Neo Vedanta, is used to communicate that the nondual essence of *Vedanta*, called *advaita*, has been reclaimed in this age. This is its newest expression on earth, taken from ancient times when it was purely expressed by the *rishis*, and presented by a fully illumined soul (*nityasiddha*) of today in the form of Swami Vivekananda. This facet is the first of five presented on the chart that accompanies this article. Truth, in India, has been considered timeless, thus eternal in all cycles of time (*mahayugas*), no matter how many times they get repeated. Some opine that truth in the form of scripture simply recurs throughout history. Others insist that it comes from the finest intellects of mankind. Others propose that it comes from the highest aspect of God in Form, namely *Ishvara/Ishvari*. But the illumined seers of India conclude that it does not come and go at all, but is ever present; it even exists in seed form at the end of a long cycle of manifestation, i.e., *Mahapralaya*. If such is the case — and all four of these perspectives have validity — Truth is certainly far beyond what people of this day and time are calling it, such as "your truth and my truth." It is wiser to simply conclude that there is relative truth and Absolute Truth, and to keep quiet about the latter until you experience it first-hand.

To shed Light on the Absolute Truth is not an easy task, especially in this world. Societies, nations, and religions are all fighting over the many forms of relative truth, and scarcely ever seek or feel attracted to what is beyond it. That would require conscious formlessness, and most beings not only cannot comprehend that, but they are afraid of it as well. Therefore, Swami Vivekananda took recourse to the ancients who gained illumination along the spiritual path, called the "razor's-edged path." As he stated: *"This state of society exists not on account of religion, but because that religion has not been applied to society as it should have been. This I am ready to prove from our old books, every word of it. This is what I teach and this is what we must struggle all our lives to carry out. But it will take time, a long time to study."*

Fortunately, Vedanta has its qualified aspect (*visishtadvaita*) to study and implement into life while the *advaitic* element in it matures and comes forward. This aspect also received the light of Swami Vivekananda's mind when he was present on earth, in the body. The *Jnana Yoga* pathway forms a large part of this area, where beings who are returning to memory of the intrinsic connec-

Parliament of Religions, 1893, Chicago

tion between *Brahman* and *Atman* can qualify themselves over time. The Order which he founded has an intense presence that is focused upon *jnanam*, and aspirants can always find teachers who are ready and able to clarify the presentation of ancient wisdom for the modern seeker. The practice of the other three main yogas, namely *bhakti, karma,* and *raja (dhyanam)*, complement the path of wisdom, enriching all aspects of universal yoga immensely. As Vivekananda foresaw and encouraged: *"I want to give Truth dry hard reason, softened in the sweetest syrup of love, and made spicy with intense work, and cooked in the kitchen of Yoga so that even a baby can easily digest it."* Here, in this single sentence, all four of the Great Yogas (*chaturdasya yoga*) are mentioned. What better way could there be to cast light upon Truth than through this timeless, eternal method?

Back to *Advaita*, in India there is still a large group of beings and the path of an *Avatar* from age to age. Sri Krishna told this secret to Arjuna several millennia prior to Lord Buddha's emanation in India, and Jesus' incarnation in the middle East, along with the secret of the sunlit and moonlit pathways for transmigrating creatures that is available at the beginning of each long cycle of time. The ridiculous notion of there being only one incarnation of God is both untenable and unacceptable. As Sri Krishna once told his disciple, Uddhava, pointing at a fruit tree, *"There are as many incarnations of God as fruits on that tree, Uddhava."* Beings who are in the know of the incarnation's appearance on the earth scene from age to age are called *Ishwarakotis*. They trace the path of the incarnation (Avataravada) when they are disembodied, and take on a birth to be with Him/Her in each of His/Her assumed lifetimes.

As for Swami Vivekananda, it fell to him to introduce this

> "I scarcely find any other God than the majestic form of my own Self. The eternal, the infinite, the omnipresent, the omniscient, is a principle, not a person. You, I, and everyone are but embodiments of that principle. The more of this infinite principle is embodied in a person, the greater is he, and all in the end will be the perfect embodiment of That and thus will be one, as they are now, essentially." Swami Vivekananda

who retain interest in this most subtle aspect of living philosophy, and the clarification that a Great Soul like Vivekananda brings to it is most welcome to them. For the rest of the world, and countries whose populace has not yet developed interest that goes beyond morality in/as religion, nonduality will have to edge its way in gradually, in somewhat clandestine fashion. As the swami wrote in the late 1800's, *"I will compare Truth to a corrosive substance of infinite power. It burns its way in wherever it falls – in soft substance at once, hard granite slowly, but it must."* The "hard granite" of belief in fundamentalist-influenced doctrines has caused most beings to accept outright the apparent difference between God and mankind, when such does not exist.

In *Advaita*, when one prays, he/she prays as God, not as one praying to God, for there is no God separate from the Self. Thus, the swami stated: *"I am a Vedantist; Satchitananda – Existence-Knowledge-Bliss Absolute – is my God; I scarcely find any other God than the majestic form of my own Self. The eternal, the infinite, the omnipresent, the omniscient, is a principle, not a person. You, I, and everyone are but embodiments of that principle. The more of this infinite principle is embodied in a person, the greater is he, and all in the end will be the perfect embodiment of That and thus will be one, as they are now essentially. This is all there is of religion, and the practice of it is through this feeling of Oneness that is love."* Until such divine intimacy is understood philosophically, practiced seamlessly, and realized ultimately, nonduality as the *"religion of the future"* will not manifest here. Only a few, rare souls will gain samadhi and merge with Brahman in inexpressible Bliss.

The second of the five chosen aspects of Swamiji's Neo-Vedanta has to do with helping beings learn about both the return important subject to both East and West, another unenviable task for the *Avatar's* messenger. For, in the West, as has been previously mentioned, narrow Christian fundamentalists had already seized upon the "my religion is the only way" perspective, and the Judaic faith did not accept that God incarnated in a form at all, other than as a messenger or a prophet. Back in India, and though religion there was open-minded and kind to the role and existence of incarnations, different factions such as sects, cults, sampradayas, and such, had begun to cling to their own Ideal, and worshipped only the incarnations that came from their specific lineage (like some schools of Vaisnavism). They could not move with the changing times in this area, even when illumined souls embodied elsewhere across the subcontinent of Mother India. Since India had always seen many realized souls over lifetimes, the culture was not able to measure the difference and degree in divine manifestation between a saintly soul, a *rishi*, a seer, a *yogi*, and an *Avatar*. Just like Christ became the "only way" in Europe and America, so too was there talk about Krishna being the "only way" In India. So the two locations exchanged religious ideals, and Christ and the missionaries came East while Krishna and the fundamentalist Vaishnavas went West. Neither could take a universalist stance, like in Advaita Vedanta, so more nonproductive infighting in religious fields went on. Then Sri Ramakrishna's advent came.

At first when Vivekananda came West to share Vedanta with interested souls in England and America, he did not mention his great *guru*, and instead taught the *"principles rather than the personality."* When asked by a few deeply interested parties about his *guru*, he said that people would find out about Him in due time, but no rush was needed there, since promoting these powerful souls to

> "For the contemplative person, the yoga of meditation (Raja Yoga), for the devout, the yoga of worship (Bhakti Yoga), for the active, the yoga of selfless works (Karma Yoga), and for the studious and discriminating, the yoga of Wisdom (Jnana Yoga) — all to be mastered and combined by sincere and striving aspirants. This was to be called Maha Yoga, Integral Yoga, Synthesis of Yoga, Purna Yoga, etc., by teachers who came after Swami Vivekananda's time."

individual nations and beings often brought the ideals They taught down, compromising the teachings due to personality worship. Nevertheless, where so many souls are "wired," or programmed, as it were, to progress via the path of *bhakti* (devotion) in this world, the introduction of an incomparable Lover of Divine Reality would definitely be extremely beneficial, and would cause so much growth among them. As Swami Vivekananda was to put it:

"To put the Hindu ideas into English and then to make out of dry philosophy, intricate mythology, and queer startling psychology a religion that shall be easy, simple, popular, and at the same time meet the requirements of the highest mind is a task that only those can understand who have attempted it. The abstract Advaita must become living – poetic – in everyday life; out of hopelessly intricate mythology must come concrete moral forms; and out of bewildering yogi-ism must come the most practical and scientific psychology – and all this must be put in a form so that a child may grasp it."

This quote of Swamiji's actually refers to the four ancient yogas taught in India since the earliest of times, which is the third highlight of his Neo Vedanta listed on the chart inset (page 13). In the Bhagavad Gita, Sri Krishna calls them *Chaturdasya Yogas*. But so long a time has passed since the teaching has been emphasized that, again, it fell to Swami Vivekananda to reach deep into the fathomless ocean of India's *Sanatana Dharma* and pull it/them forth, wring them out to rid them of the encrustations of ages, and present them to humanity again — all under the banner of a freshly revised *Advaita Vedanta*.

Yoga reduced to physical postures and breathing exercises is a caricature of itself, but Yoga taught and practiced in its original eight-limbed form is the supreme method for transformation, and represents true *sadhana* in a world full of faith and grace-based religions that seldom advise recourse to self-effort leading to formlessness, i.e., leading beyond form and heaven. Yoga aligned with Vedanta is simply one of the best hybrids of mind-clearing philosophy available to mankind, the world over. And Yoga viewed through the lens of *Advaita* reveals the true meaning of its name, Union – Union with Divine Reality.

Envision, then, not one, but four timeless yogas brought back into prominence in this age, this *Kali Yuga*, this age of darkness. For the contemplative person, the yoga of meditation (*Raja Yoga*), for the devout, the yoga of worship (*Bhakti Yoga*), for the active, the yoga of selfless works (*Karma Yoga*), and for the studious and discriminating, the yoga of Wisdom (*Jnana Yoga*) – all to be mastered and combined by sincere and striving aspirants. This was to be called *Maha Yoga*, Integral Yoga, Synthesis of Yoga, *Purna Yoga*, etc., by teachers who came after Swami Vivekananda's time, after his brief 39 years in the body. To quote his vision for its maturation and realization, he stated: "*The older Teachers were rather one-sided, while the teaching of this new Incarnation is that the best point of Yoga, Devotion, Knowledge, and Work must be combined now so as to form a new society. This is the new religion of this age – the synthesis of Yoga, Knowledge, Devotion, and Work – the propagation of Knowledge and Devotion down to the very lowest, without distinction of age or sex. The previous Incarnations were all right, but they have been synthesized in the person of Ramakrishna. We now have a new India, with its new God, new religion, and new Vedas. When, O Lord, shall our land be free from this eternal dwelling upon the past? All great Personalities should be duly honored, but homage should be paid now to Sri Ramakrishna.*"

More can be said on this important subject, and the enlightening tenets of it duly practiced, but the tone and tenor of Swami's quote above brings up a fourth aspect of the Neo Vedanta — the powerful import of India's timeless scriptures and their unique teachings. In other words, where can one find spirituality in this world? Religion and philosophy can be found, expressed in churches, temples, and educational institutions, but spirituality has mainly to do with what is other-worldly, the "*open space beyond religion,*" to quote Lex Hixon. Specifically, it focuses on transcending rebirth in various forms which are assumed in worlds lying in inner and outer space, and merging the embodied soul into the ocean of timeless, deathless Awareness that is formless. Thus, we find in India the only collection of nondual scriptures which both explain the secret of this "Oneness," and describe — as best as words can tell — how to reach It and what It consists of.

Further, these represent the testament of the many realized souls who attained to It, this "Enlightenment" that is cherished above and beyond dualistic religious experience and intellectual philosophical knowledge. Profound words for it abound as well, such as *nirvana*, *nirvikalpa*, *satori*, *asamprajnata*, *kaivalya*, *moksha*, *mukti*, *prajnaparam*, *sattasamanya*, *samadhi*, and others. To be certain, to release the small self from finite lifetimes constrained by time, space, pleasure, heavenly enjoyments, all bodies, human or celestial, is not the goal of human beings, nor is it pointed to as the purpose of life by religious traditions or their scriptures. Yet, it was Sri Ramakrishna's uncompromising position, that "*He is born to no ultimate purpose, who, having been granted the precious boon of a human body, is unable to realize God in this very lifetime.*"

In the *Gospel of Sri Ramakrishna*, He is quoted to have said, "*It is my most mature opinion, that a man abides at the nitya (eternal level), comes down to the Lila (the level of sportive play), then returns to the Nitya to merge.*" It is passing strange that, though the Great Master sometimes spoke of *maya*, the inscrutable level of limited existence fraught with obscuration and distortion, He, Himself remained above it, and could see through it. Sri Sarada Devi said, that of all the beings in the world, only Sri Ramakrishna was able to see through maya. He *"watched it from a safe distance,"* as He said, and from there was able to draw striving and suffering souls up and out of it.

This involves the fifth of the Neo Vedanta tenets listed on the chart under study here, the innate perfection of the human soul. Swami Vivekananda was on hand after the Master's *Mahasamadhi* to remind souls, in the East and the West, of their inherent divinity, and thus reverse the ugly trend of fallen Christianity whose priests were telling its followers that they were sinners. One can imagine the relief mingled with wonder at this "good news" the illumined swami brought to a benighted Western world, whose main religion had misinterpreted the message of Jesus so blatantly as to have it become the very devil that the Bible itself preached against.

As to Western man's attraction for higher knowledge, by the second of Swami Vivekananda's visit to the West and America, he was already noticing a transformation in the thinking process of both intelligent thinkers and sincere seekers in England and America, and in the overall antagonistic religious mood of the people against such liables and indignities as the Christian priest class had been handing out. Thus, he wrote to one of his supporters in India from America:*"Sober minded men here have become disgusted with their superstitious religions and are looking forward to India for new light. How eagerly they take in any little bit of the grand thoughts of the holy Vedas, which resist and are unharmed by the terrible onslaughts of modern science. The theories of creation out of nothing, or a created soul, and of the big tyrant of a God sitting on a throne in a place called heaven, and of eternal hell-fires, have disgusted all the educated; and the noble thoughts of the Vedas about the eternity of creation and of the soul, they are imbibing fast in one shape or another. Within fifty years the educated world will come to believe in the eternity of both soul and creation, and in God as our highest and perfect nature, as taught in our holy Vedas. Even now their learned priests are interpreting the Bible that way."*

The perfection of mankind's nature is an eternal fact. Mankind's disbelief in this principle is due to it never being taught in religion. It was seldom even postulated in Western philosophy. Man, himself, failed to realize it due to lack of faith in it and himself. Constantly seeing all the imperfections in his outer form, and in nature, he only continued to emphasize all the more his identification with both of these (the body and matter), and thereby blinded himself to his changeless Essence, his *svarupa*. As Swami Vivekananda said it, directly: *"You are God, I am God, and man is God. It is this God manifested through humanity who is doing everything in this world. Is there a different God sitting high up somewhere? God can only be known in and through mankind. Vibrations of light are everywhere, even in the darkest corners, but it is in a lamp that it becomes visible. Man is that lamp."*

New Lamps for Old

New light for this age, coming from those eternally Great Lamps who are *"God walking around on two legs,"* is fast becoming known now as the "New Dispensation" and the "Neo Vedanta." In this world, beings wait centuries, even millennia, for its return. The grogginess that clings to the mind after waking from sleep is

Swami Vivekananda with other attendees of the Parliament of Religions

similar to the lack of recognition that living beings suffer when Consciousness unmasks itself once an age, and stands there fully revealed in the august form of a Sri Ramakrishna and a Swami Vivekananda. And this world has now seen both!

Sri Ramakrishna is the *Avatar* of this *yuga*. Sri Sarada Devi is the Divine Mother of the Universe in human form. Swami Vivekananda is the perfect man, and the *Avatar's* messenger. A host of other luminaries, both monastic and householders, have accompanied him to earth. Millions of beings are now becoming aware of Them, and are taking refuge in this incomparable Ideal, the likes of Whom have never appeared with such full and unbridled spiritual force (*Shakti*) as recently. As one beautiful spiritual hymn from India puts it, *"Bubbling up from the very heart of Bengal, the sacred Ganges is streaming forth compassion once again. Take heed and come forth, all ye who would drink of its sanctifying waters of Eternal Life. From birth to death, and death to birth goes the soul, driven inexorably by the burning fire of unfulfilled desires. Come friend, the world is but a mirage, and you have exhausted yourself chasing illusions. One dip in the river of Ramakrishna will refresh you completely, and remove all sorrows and anxieties. The river of Ramakrishna is a powerful tributary which flows eternally to the boundless ocean of divine bliss. So renounce vain pursuits and hollow attachments and rush to the boat of His hallowed Feet."*

Babaji Bob Kindler is the Spiritual Director of the SRV Associations with its two centers in Hawaii and Oregon. A teacher of religion and spirituality and a prolific author, his books include The Avadhut, Twenty-Four Aspects of Mother Kali, Ten Divine Articles of Sri Durga, Swami Vivekananda Vijnanagita, Sri Sarada Vijnanagita, An Extensive Anthology of Sri Ramakrishna's Stories, A Quintessential Yoga Vasishtha, Reclaiming Kundalini Yoga, Cosmic Quintuplications, Jnana Matra, Manasana, Footfalls of the Indian Rishis, and others. Founder and Artistic Director of Jai Ma Music, he is also an accomplished musician, recording artist, and composer, who has produced over twenty-five albums of instrumental and devotional music to date.

✢ Christ the Sannyasin ✢
The Key Renunciation Teachings of Jesus of Nazareth

"Do not suppose that I have come to bring peace to the earth. I did not come to bring peace, but a sword. I have come to turn a man against his father, a daughter against her mother, a daughter-in-law against her mother-in-law. A man's enemies will be the members of his own household. Anyone who loves father or mother more than me is not worthy of me; anyone who loves their son or daughter more than me is not worthy of me. Whoever does not take up their cross and follow me is not worthy of me. Whoever finds their life will lose it, and whoever loses their life for my sake will find it."
Matthew 10:34-36

"None of you can be My disciple who does not give up all his own possessions."
Luke 14:33

"And the man said: 'Lord, first let me bury my father; then I will follow you.' But Jesus replied, 'Let the dead bury their dead; you come with me to proclaim the Kingdom of God.'"
Matthew 8:22

"Birds have nests and foxes have holes, but the son of man hath no place to lay his head." Matthew 8:18

"For, what will it profit a man, if he should gain the whole world but lose his soul?"
Luke 22:27

"And everyone who has left houses or brothers or sisters or father or mother or children or farms for My name's sake, will receive many times as much, and will inherit eternal life." Matthew 19:29

"Guard what has been entrusted to you, avoiding the world and its empty chatter and the opposing arguments of what is falsely called 'knowledge.'"
Timothy 6:20

"Seek ye first the kingdom of God, and his righteousness, and all things shall be added unto thee." Matt. 6:33

"Render unto Caesar what is Caesar's, but give unto the Lord what is the Lord's...."
Spiritual things, such as worship and obedience, give these to God; for these He demands from you as his right, and by so doing you will offend neither God nor Caesar." Mark 12:17

Reverend Chris VonLobedan

THE UNIVERSAL & THE SPECIFIC

In Issue 34 I developed the idea of a "personal worldview" to describe an individual's perspective intrinsic to a time and place. The cultural and historical context of a person's experience is foundational to how they understand or articulate their understanding of the nature of things. Religious formulations that inform this perspective reflect a cultural heritage. Religious or philosophical influences become amalgamated into a personal worldview. Other factors pertain to this process, but for the sake of brevity, the vocabulary and subsequent formulations of religious insight are objectively truncated by personal experience of a historical nature.

I presented some of the influences that shaped my thinking. These teachers, mentors, and studies are reflected in the ideas presented. My worldview is the product of others in this sense, and the product of an objective reality to which I am subject. To some degree these various sources have been combined into a personal perspective because of my life experience.

In issue 36 I explored the function of duality and the idea that the dialogue with other perspectives creates a "growing edge" to the historical present. Our understanding naturally tends to evolve with new insights. I recognized a dialogical nature of experience. Polemics characterize awareness and are existential in how awareness functions. The seer and the seen, the self and the other, are examples of how duality is intrinsic to awareness. Dependent co-origination is an Eastern concept that I believe helps describe how duality is intrinsic to consciousness. The unifying fact of experience could be a phenomenology of perception structured by polemics or duality. The subject as observer and that which is observed or considered is productive of awareness. An ego or sense of self exists in relation to observations and considerations.

In order to explore my understanding of Universalism it is helpful to keep these previous submissions to Nectar in mind. I am Christian by profession and practice, but many of the influences that have contributed to my worldview originated in other cultures and historical circumstances. My understanding of a Christian Universalism could be considered corrupt because my thoughts are not solely formed from within the dogma and teachings ascribed to Christianity.

"My" Background

My parents left their religious roots behind in a move west to California when I was an infant, Mother's family were Methodists from a small town in Wisconsin, and father's family was Catholic from the city. Religious interests were prompted in me at the time of my father's death in my late teens. The College of Marin was close to our home, and I met John Bruce. John provided a reading list on Mysticism unrelated to the courses he taught. He eventually became my mentor. John and his wife Eleanor re-parented me.

John had adopted the spiritual name Zero following the experience of Absolute Nothingness. Zero poses a unique empirical starting point to acknowledge a Universal experience that many sages, saints and gurus share. Zero was a Christian by profession, but over time we studied any number of teachings on Mysticism. The experience of Nothingness presents a foundation to structure and supports an interfaith dialogue that seems unrestricted by cultural and historical forms. At one time he said, "You might as well work within the Christian tradition, it is most popular here." Zero clearly saw any number of traditions address Mystical theology.

Masao Abe also influenced my ideas in several significant ways. He taught over several terms at the Graduate Theological Union in Berkley. He later lived at my home in Coos Bay, Oregon, and taught in the Pacific Northwest for about a year. In a lecture at the Graduate Theological Union he presented a short paper entitled "A Dog Named Ralph." The paper described the dog as a mammal, as a creature, as a being on Earth, as a creation of God. He pointed out the larger categories of thought that encompass a thing that can culminate in God. Then the essay retraces its steps back to the dog, but a very specific dog, Ralph. Subsumptive logic was a phrase that described the larger categories of being that subsume other specific ideas or things.

The point of the lecture was to recognize that the nature of things is comprised of distinct elements as the self-expression of God. It is not mammals or animals or larger categories of being, but the nature of things must contain Ralph as a unique form in time and place. "The very hairs on your head are accounted for" acknowledges a similar idea in the Bible. Masao had a very developed understanding of religious apology and reconciled his understanding of the nature of things to Absolute Nothingness. Paradoxical and contradictory formulations offered a view of transcendence that reconciled immanence to an ineffable experience of Absolute Nothingness.

Another significant event occurred while on a trip with friends. I stayed back to read and reflect in a dorm room in Chico, California. I might have been dozing but found myself confronted by a person who was standing before me. I was perplexed by his manner. He was very insightful and lent me the impression that he understood all of the foibles and characteristics that had occurred over the course of my lifetime. The entire culmination of actions that had constituted my experiences seemed available to him. His compassion, acceptance, and love perplexed me. I asked, "Who are you?" He said "Jesus Christ" and I thought, "That makes perfect sense, of course Jesus would be like that." I next said, "What should I do?" "Do whatever you want" was his reply. Given the implication that I was free to choose, I thought, "Well, I want a piece of your action." I enjoyed his company in adoration and devotion, then later found myself alone in the dorm again.

The Contrast Between the Universal and Specific

The specificity of the individual is an aspect of experience that gets relegated to being inconsequential or delusional in some of the arguments that support Universalism Contrasts between religious traditions in the treatment of the ego or self. They can present a stumbling block in interfaith dialogue. A Hegelian style polemic helps explicate these contrasting teleological perspectives. Presuming the ego as an enduring entity in Western theology can be juxtaposed with the ego as illusion in Eastern teachings. Abe advanced a philosophical position that was non-theistic and reconciled the present moment of concrete reality of experience to the self-expression of Absolute Nothingness. His work presented this rare quality of experience as not simply the absence of cognitive processes or sense of self. Masao consequently or necessarily taught the "via negativa" as a more accurate approach to understand the nature of things.

The real constraints of time and place, a culture, a legacy, a teleos, are more than just subjective qualifications of experience. As a point of reference, these factors are amalgamated into the limitations of the present experience. We are confronted by the "real" problem of living in the circumstances that both confine and give expression to being. Nishida Kitaro used the term "place" to acknowledge this dimension of experience. These are the predicates of a dialectical treatment of awareness that mutually become resolved into Absolute Nothingness. Subjective and objective qualifications of experience are mutually negating.

Mysticism in its most refined expressions also avoids the limitations imposed by the dialectics of reason. Mystical Theism employs God as a moral and creative source of this process that cannot be objectified. For those that have not been subject to the experience of Absolute Nothingness, this resolution to the paradoxes of awareness tends to be reductionist. In contemporary Western culture nihilism and materialism have become more prominent. Subjective dimensions of experience present an unresolvable contradiction of consciousness except in cases of rare forms of direct experience. The "place" of Nishida's logic is not an object, and the subject cannot be objectified. Contradictory or paradoxical formulations are common in Nishida's teachings, and the Kyoto School of Philosophy. "Because it is personal it is Universal and it is not Universal because it is personal, thats what makes it Universal," are common.

Christ's Claim Upon a Person

The foundation of paradox provides a contradictory support for Universalism. Mathematics, the common patterns that structure nature, archetypes that structure human experience, all acknowledge a unity behind experience. Universalism founded upon the present moment as a consistent factor in experience simultaneously appears unique and personal. The processes of change and multiplicity might be an anti-thesis to a type of Oneness beyond things, but appears limited as an argument for Universalism. Absolute Nothingness proposes a rare fact of experience unencumbered by dichotomies, but avoids a nihilistic contemporary perspective on the nature of existence.

The intimate and personal nature of Christian experience accommodates the exclusive or individual dimension of revelation. Amalgamating all things into God is a typical way to address the Universal. *"In God we live and move and have our being,"* yet we exist separate in the world and are part of it. The paradox of trinitarian formulations help resolve this cognitive conundrum. The experiential insights of Christian mysticism explore the self-negating quality of the transcendent as a foundation of experience. In this respect the paradox of trinitarian doctrine help reconcile that which cannot be objectified and our subjective existence.

The very intimate nature of a "personal relationship" with Jesus is not atypical. Many share the experience of an encounter or vision of Christ as a foundation of their faith. Most Christians structure their worldview around ideas like the preservation of the ego, a heavenly reward, and being reunited with those that have already passed. Nominally we enjoy a continuity of experience in time with the sense of continuity that constitutes a lifetime, and this is advanced in teachings of the afterlife as well. Christian teachings place Jesus both in time and outside of time as the self-expression of God at the act of creation. The author of creation and the assurance of our eternal rest is a type of formulation common to contemporary Christianity.

Religious worldviews commonly recognize that the ego or person will be constrained to a future determined by present predilections or past events. This process is mitigated by grace in many traditions, so a strict mechanism of consequence is not the only process involved. Judgement day, redemption and grace, all have their place in the consequential outcomes presented by Christianity. Religious worldviews present a hierarchy of being that qualifies human experience. The coarse man, as contrasted with the virtuous one, acknowledges moral and spiritual qualifications to experience. In Eastern thought, the Bodhisattva vow presents a type of loving concern that would conform our nature to an intrinsic goodness that is the foundation of things. As a prison Chaplain, soteriological concerns present a backdrop for many involved in religious practice.

"The Fall" or sin, is presented as the cause of separation in Christian epistemology. The assumed continuity of self-awareness in time is a common presumption of Christian formulations. Within the symbolic language of tradition, we are products of the rebellion represented by eating the apple; our way back is barred, and our way forward is determined by the actor that is God's self-expression in Jesus Christ. Preserving the intimate nature of a specific, historic, and personal quality to religious truth is a dimension of Christianity that begs accommodation in the treatment of Universalism. Mysticism and contradiction is intrinsic to this accommodation in a reciprocity encountered as a paradox.

Reverend Chris von Lobedan has served Shutter Creek Correctional Institution in Coos Bay Oregon for 17 years. His Doctor of Ministry and Master of Divinity were awarded from San Francisco Theological Seminary. He was the pastor of the First Presbyterian Church of Coos Bay for 13 years. He was recognized with the Transitional Services Employee of the Year award for his work in the religious reentry program Home for Good. He has worked extensively inside his institution to train volunteers to understand the importance of assisting those with whom they work with faith-based assistance as they transition from prison. He has brought a specific faith-traditions approach to that training and been one of the leaders in the development of Home for Good.

TURNING WITHIN
Where There is Peace, There is God

There could be two modes in which a person may live. He may think and act as an extrovert or as an introspective. Spiritual life, however, begins with turning within, by becoming introspective. Says Swami Vivekananda:

"There is one impulse in our mind which says do. Behind it rises another voice which says do not. There is one set of ideas in our mind which is always struggling to get outside through the channels of the senses, and behind that, although it may be thin and weak, there is an infinitely small voice which says, do not go outside. The two beautiful Sanskrit words for these phenomena are 'Pravritti' and 'Nivritti', 'circling forward' and 'circling inward'. It is the circling forwards which usually governs our actions. Religion begins with this circling inward. Religion begins with this 'do not'. Spirituality begins with this 'do not'. When the 'do not' is not there, religion has not begun."

Most of us are extroverts, even though we may be religious. Even when an inclination for religion seems to arise, to bud and sprout in our hearts, we continue to remain extroverts. We go on pilgrimages, read a number of scriptures, participate in holy festivals, perform religious rituals and ceremonies, but our mind still remains outgoing. We continue to be "religious extroverts" or "extrovert devotees." We just go on floating on the surface, as it were, with no depth. Authentic spiritual life has not begun for most of us who have such tendencies.

But as Swamiji has said, if we truly wish to grow spiritually, we must turn the senses inwards — must give up the tendency of the senses to run outwards. This need for turning within has also been recognized by various thinkers in modern times. The modern man has become far more extrovert than ever before. There are many more external allurements which constantly draw the mind and the senses outwards, with consequent heightened activity and restlessness. Even for a little peace of mind, "turning within," a little of that "do not" is necessary. This may not be easy in the beginning, however, for the senses accustomed to run outward, and for a restless mind unaccustomed to the introspective mode.

In recent times, a number of ashramas, foundations, religious organizations, and meditation centers have sprung up all over the world to gradually train the mind and senses to turn within. Such centers organize spiritual retreats, conferences or conventions. A spiritual retreat actually means a secluded place where individuals can go and live in solitude for a few days. But since this is often not practical nor even advisable for most people who are unaccustomed to live a solitary life; people only assemble in groups in some ashrama for a few days or hours and participate in a program of devotional singing, meditation, scriptural readings, discourses, discussions and so on.

Then there are many teachers and groups who teach meditation and conduct guided meditation classes. There are also camps and courses on yoga where an effort is made to teach an integrated way of living. But it must be remembered that turning within is not merely practicing meditation, however important it may be. And many vital instructions for an introspective life are often found missing in these meditation camps and the methods advocated therein. In contrast, when we turn to Sri Ramakrishna, the great master of the art of living an introspective life, we find that he has not described any elaborate meditation technique. He may have taught meditation to individuals, but he gave far more comprehensive instructions for turning within.

Let us study the instructions Sri Ramakrishna gave to 'M' in reply to his question: *'How, Sir, may we fix our mind on God?'* Coined in non-theological terms, this question would read, 'How can we become introspective?' It is significant that except saying that *'to meditate you should withdraw within yourself or retire into a secluded corner or to the forest,'* Sri Ramakrishna did not give detailed instructions about the technique of meditation. Instead he said: (i) Repeat God's name and sing his glories, (ii) Keep holy company, (iii) Go into solitude now and then, and (iv) discriminate between the real and unreal.

Discriminate Between the Real and the Unreal

Of the above mentioned instructions of Sri Ramakrishna, discrimination and *satsanga* or holy company condition the mind. An extrovert mind runs after external objects and urges one to engage in various activities to achieve worldly aims because it considers them real, desirable, and conducive to happiness. But when by discrimination, one is convinced of their impermanence and undesirability, of their being the cause of misery, it will not run after them anymore. Says Sri Ramakrishna:

"You should always discriminate between the Real and the unreal. God alone is real, the Eternal Substance; all else is unreal, that is, impermanent. By discriminating thus, one should shake off impermanent objects from the mind. Together with this, practice discrimination. 'Lust and gold' is impermanent. God is the only Eternal Substance. What does a man get with money? Food, clothes, and a dwelling place – nothing more. You cannot realize God with its help. Therefore money can never be the goal of life. That is the process of discrimination."

Discrimination is a very important means of developing dispassion. Unfortunately, this is not realized by many who, though practicing meditation, do not try to detach their minds from worldly objects. Unless the mind is detached from external delights and attachment to objects, individuals, and activities, it cannot remain indrawn for long. The pull of sense-attraction and urge for worldly pursuits would drive it out. This is the reason that many of us do not progress on the path of meditation in spite of many years of practice.

It may not be possible to give up our desires and ambitions all at once. The next best thing one can do in such a condition is to be satisfied with the worldly state one is in. This message is contained in Sri Ramakrishna's instructions to Adhara Sen, a Deputy Magistrate, who was aspiring for a still higher governmental post:

"Nivritti alone is good and not pravritti. Be satisfied with the job you have. People hanker after a post paying fifty or hundred rupees. You are earning three hundred rupees. You are a deputy magistrate. Is a deputy magistrate a person to be trifled with?"

We are often tempted to change our external circumstances; to seek what we think could be a better material or psychological situation. But there is no such thing as an ideal environment. But wealth, name, and fame, social status etc. can never satisfy a man. There is no limit to our desiring. It is therefore essential to put a brake on our desires and attempts at seeking a better job, a better house, a better environment or a better salary, if one really wants to become introspective.

A formula one might use to weaken the extrovert tendency and promptings of the mind is to ask oneself during such promptings: "Can I do without it?" Can I do without the object, activity or pleasure for which my mind is aspiring? Let us take a concrete example. Suppose I get a desire for a new fountain pen or a pair of new shoes. Let me ask before going for it: 'Can I do without it? Do I already have a pen or a pair of shoes? Do I really need a new one? Or a spare one? Is it not a fact that many spare items go on accumulating and demand time and energy for their maintenance?' The same question can be posed when there is an urge to embark upon some activity: 'Can I do without it? Can it be postponed?' Try to reduce your requirements and extrovert activities and simplify your life. To remain contented with our present socio-economic status is the first step towards *nivritti*.

The conversation which followed Sri Ramakrishna's preliminary remarks to Adhar Sen provides further guidelines for turning inwards. "One may learn to reduce one's wants and desires, but should one not strive for one's livelihood?" In answer to this anticipated question, Sri Ramakrishna told the story of a young sannyasin who was ignorant of worldly matters and had gone to beg his food for the first time. A young daughter of the household came out to give him alms. The sannyasin turned to her mother and asked whether the girl had abscesses on her chest. The mother explained that God had given the girl breasts to nurse her child when she would become a mother. Hearing this, the sannyasin said that in that case he need not worry about food. "*He who has created me will certainly feed me.*"

To strive for more wealth and property, higher salary and position in society for oneself and one's near and dear ones may be selfish, but is there any harm in building schools and colleges, hospitals and dispensaries, and in engaging in other philanthropic activities? According to Sri Ramakrishna, *daya* or compassion is better than *maya* or attachment for one's family only. The former leads to liberation and the latter to bondage. But even these altruistic activities fall under the category of *pravritti*, or extrovert tendencies. Shambu Mallik wanted to build schools and hospitals with the money he had amassed. Sri Ramakrishna asked him, instead, to pray to God and strive for devotion and vision of God.

Lord Krishna has repeatedly referred to one technique in the Bhagavad Gita: giving up all will and desires, *sarvasankalpa sannyasa*. Hundreds of ideas, desires, and ambitions arise in our mind. Most of them are weak. However, certain desires are strong, and when we add our will to those desires, they take the form of *sankalpa*: a resolve which prompts us to fulfill it. A yogi on the contrary does not unite his will with the various desires. Consequently, due to lack of their being fulfilled, the desires die away. Besides, every action we perform is bound to have a reaction. Every ball we throw, as it were, is bound to bounce back. This chain of action and reaction continues to expand and extend till we are caught in a net of our own outward activities, good or bad.

There is a whole lot of difference between the activities of an extrovert and the same activities performed by an introspective person. This would become clear if we were to live in solitude and consciously make an effort to withdraw from outward activities for a length of time. Such a person can remain active and at the same time deeply rooted in the innermost self. He can at will withdraw from activity and also engage in intense activity, if required. This is the ideal as defined by Swami Vivekananda often:

"The ideal man is he who, in the midst of the greatest silence and solitude, finds the intensest activity, and in the midst of the intensest activity finds the silence and solitude of the desert. He has learnt the secret of restraint; he has controlled himself. He goes through the streets of a big city, with all its traffic, and his mind is as calm as if he were in a cave where not a sound could reach him; and he is intensely working all the time." For this ideal, an introspective mode must be diligently cultivated.

Satsanga or holy company is another means of conditioning the mind for an introspective mode. According to Sri Ramakrishna, mind is like a white cloth. It takes on the color of the dye in which it is dipped. If it is placed in the company of extroverts, it will become extrovert. If it is placed in the company of all-renouncing introspective saints and recluses, it will also turn inwards. Holy company convinces an individual who comes in it that true peace and happiness is possible only in turning within, in seeking unity in diversity and not in pursuing the multi-directed desires of mind.

Sri Ramakrishna has laid great stress on living in solitude for as long as one can conveniently do. He said:

"By meditating on God in solitude the mind acquires knowledge, dispassion, and devotion. But the very same mind goes downwards if it dwells in the world. In the world there is only one thought: 'lust and gold.'" And:

"The world is water and the mind milk. If you pour milk into water they become one; you cannot find pure milk any more. But turn the milk into curd and churn it into butter. Then, when that butter is placed in water, it will float. So, practice spiritual discipline in solitude and obtain the butter of knowledge and love. Even if you keep that butter in the water of the world the two will not mix. The butter will float."

Solitude cuts out external stimuli and prevents the mind from indulging in sense pleasures. The mind naturally becomes quiet. One also gets an opportunity to observe the workings of the mind when the turmoil of the external world is absent.

In solitude we are forced to be away from the objects of our attachment and psychological dependence. None of our relatives, friends, and foes, with whom we relate ourselves with love or hatred, are there. Solitude thus gives us an opportunity to live without those on whom we depend, or those who depend on us. In our ignorance and folly we think that we cannot live without this or that thing, person or activity, or that such and such a person cannot live without us. Living in solitude helps in destroying this false notion. After a period of retreat we realize that neither we nor others have suffered much by this separation. We learn that none is indispensable. We find that in our absence the world does not go to pieces or come to a standstill. Our false sense of self-importance, our impure ego, thereby gets the much needed blow.

During such retreats into solitude, we must not engage in our accustomed activities. This helps in breaking the automation into which we are often liable to fall due to our routine lives. There are no newspaper, radio, TV, and visitors to bring to us the gossip of the world. Living in solitude thus prevents the worldly and extrovert tendency of the mind from becoming deep-rooted, and helps us to turn the mind inward.

> "The world is water and the mind milk. If you pour milk into water they become one; you cannot find pure milk any more. But turn the milk into curd and churn it into butter. Then, when that butter is placed in water, it will float. So, practice spiritual disciplines in solitude and obtain the butter of knowledge."

Solitude is also important for concentration of mind. A restless mind cannot think uninterruptedly of God. Its restlessness must be reduced at least to some extent if one wants to meditate well. The mind gets restless either due to external sensory stimuli, or due to thought-waves arising out of the store of past impressions in the subconscious mind. If the external sensory stimuli are not stopped, they not only disturb the mind but also produce fresh impressions or *samskaras*. So it is advisable for one to live in such an environment where the external stimuli are minimum. Then the problem caused by the internal stimuli arising out of past impressions alone remains for the spiritual aspirant to deal with. And if these impressions are noble, controlling them will not be difficult.

These are some "negative" measures one must take to turn inwards. But merely negative means are not enough. Sri Ramakrishna therefore advocates some very important spiritual practices.

"*Repeating God's Name and singing His glories*" is the first means told by Sri Ramakrishna when "M" asks him: "*How, Sir, may we fix our mind on God?*" This technique has been recommended even by Patanjali, the great exponent of Yoga. He says that the thought waves can be controlled by the repetition of "Om," which symbolizes the name of God, and by thinking on its meaning. By this the mind becomes introspective and the obstacles (in the path of Yoga) are removed.

Japa is the traditional way of turning the mind within, and has been emphasized in all religious systems. But all the saints and sages, teachers and acharyas, emphasize that it must be done with some amount of concentration.

How does *japa* make the mind introspective? According to Sri Ramakrishna, "*Sandhya merges into Gayatri and Gayatri into Om.*" This is the process of verbal convergence which is the first step, preliminary to mental concentration. *Japa* leads to *vak-ektanatha*. Before our mind can learn to flow towards one object, our speech must learn to flow towards, and merge into, one word. Done with concentration, *japa* has a tremendous capacity of cutting down the multiplicity and diversity of speech or spoken thought. We either think in forms, or in words and language. Both are connected, interdependent. Hence it is quite reasonable and scientific that *japa* should help in the introspection of mind.

To the repetition of God's name, Sri Ramakrishna has added another technique: singing God's glories. It is a well known fact that music has a tremendous effect upon the human psyche, and Sri Ramakrishna knew it very well. Musical recitation of the glories and life-history of the incarnations of God draws our minds inwards as nothing else. Sri Ramakrishna was himself a very good singer, and would often go into deep ecstasy while singing the glories of God.

Thus, in Sri Ramakrishna's short reply to "M's question, we find a comprehensive recipe for turning the mind within. Discrimination and solitude help in withdrawing the mind from its extrovert tendencies, holy company conditions the mind for introspection, and *japa* and singing God's glories turns it within. A person accustomed to these can easily succeed in meditation.

(This article has been reprinted with the permission of Vedanta Keshari)

A former editor of the Vedanta Keshari, and previously of the Ramakrishna Mission Home of Service, Swami Brameshananda is a senior monk of the Ramakrishna Order and until recently was the Secretary of the Ramakrishna Mission Ashram in Chandigarh, India. Over the years his writings in Hindi and English have appeared in several journals, including Prabuddha Bharata, Vedanta Keshari, and Nectar of Nondual Truth. He specializes in themes related to Jainism. He is now retired and is living an inner, contemplative life in Varanasi.

Wisdom Facets From the Gem of Truth

Sri Ramakrishna

Holy Mother, Sri Sarada Devi

"Schools of Consciousness"

"It is enough to believe that all is possible in God's creation. The facets of God's creation are infinite. Sometimes I see that His creation is saturated with Consciousness, just like the earth is soaked with water in the rainy season. The earth and its beings are conscious on account of God's Consciousness. I find that this Consciousness even wriggles about in the form of small fish, as it were."

(The Gospel of Sri Ramakrishna)

Be Thou a Vijnani

"The vijnani sees that Brahman is immovable and actionless, like Mount Sumeru. The universe consists of the three gunas — sattva, rajas, and tamas. They are in Brahman, but Brahman is unattached. The vijnani further sees that what is Brahman is the Bhagavan, the personal God. He who is beyond the three gunas is the Bhagavan, with His six supernatural powers called living beings, the universe, mind, intelligence, love, renunciation, and knowledge."

(The Gospel of Sri Ramakrishna)

Moving Heads

"I see the indivisible Satchidananda both inside and outside. It has merely assumed this sheath of the body as an external support. And I see all of you as so many sheaths, but the heads are moving."

(The Gospel of Sri Ramakrishna)

Constancy & Transparency

"If a man practices spiritual disciplines before his death, and if he gives up his body praying to God and meditating on Him, when will sin ever be able to touch him? So pray to Him earnestly. He will tell you everything."

(The Gospel of Sri Ramakrishna)

All the Yogas, Together Now

"After you gain your initiation, it is then that you can do work in the right spirit. You will be able to accomplish your duties well. No sin will be able to attach itself to you again. Every day, after bathing, offer your salutations to the Master, and remember Him in the course of every piece of work that you do. This will fulfill the purpose of your japa and meditation. And when you find the time, pray to him earnestly. If duties begin to take up too much time, do what you can in the early hours prior to others rising from bed. Remember that japa and meditation are meant for realizing God. It is only because you have received God's Grace that you have come to me."

(The Compassionate Mother)

Affections and Austerities

"Through japa and austerity the bonds of karma are cut asunder. However, God cannot be realized unless through love and devotion. The power of the sense organs is subdued by japa and other disciplines. But did the cowherd boys of Vrindaban get Krishna as their own through austerities? They realized Him through ecstatic love."

(The Compassionate Mother)

Divine Mother & Divine Child

"One day in the noontime, the Master was seated on a small cot, and I was sweeping the room. There was none there besides us. I asked Him, 'Who am I to you?' He instantly replied, 'You are my blissful Divine Mother.'"

(The Compassionate Mother)

The Inner Secret of External Love

"If someone is one's very own, they remain inseparably connected over succesive cycles of time. Selfless love makes the beloved one's own forever."

(The Compassionate Mother)

Wisdom Facets From the Gem of Truth

Painting by Swami Tadatmananda

Swami Vivekananda   Disciples & Devotees of Sri Ramakrishna

Worship of Shakti is Work for Shakti

"Mother has been born to revive Shakti in India, and throughout the world. Whoever will assist in this work of the Divine Mother of the Universe will have Her Grace, and whoever will oppose it will not only 'raise a deadly enemy for nothing,' but will also lay an axe to his own prospects. We want thousands of women, thousands of men, who will spread like wildfire to do this work. It will not do to merely call Sri Ramakrishna an incarnation; we must manifest this shakti power."

(Talks with Swami Vivekananda)

In the World-Carnival, the Ego is a Cheap Prize

"This is the Truth; we are caught in a trap, and the sooner we get out, the better for us. May we not get stuck in self-imposed bondages anymore. The world is so little, life so mean a thing, existence so, so servile, that I wonder, and smile, that human beings, rational souls, should be running after this self — so mean and detestable a prize."

(Talks With Swami Vivekananda)

Selfless Works for the Self-Realization of All

"Organization has its faults no doubt, but without that, nothing can be done. No one ever succeeded in keeping society in good humor and at the same time did good works. One must work as the dictate comes from within, and then if it is right and good, society will veer around, perhaps centuries after one is dead and gone."

(Talks With Swami Vivekananda)

"All Are Fighting Over the Same Old Threadbare Rug"

"The condition of the world is pitiable. The people here cannot even dream what renunciation truly means. Luxury and sensuality have so much been eating into the vitals of the races. May God send renunciation and unworldliness into these lands."

(Talks with Swami Vivekananda)

Perfect Yourself First, Then Help Others

"Nowadays many feel that they should devote their lives to the service of mankind. I believe that this idea has taken hold of the minds of people because of the influence of modern education. The truth is, that it is not possible to do good to others until one has matured one's own character. Until this is accomplished, people make all kinds of errors. Those who have taken refuge in Brahman and received His Grace can never take a false step. Their words acts, and behavior naturally become a source of good to everyone."

(Swami Brahmananda, The Eternal Companion)

Infuse Sadhana With Power

"Power seeks channels for its manifestation and gathers force from obstructions. The mantra you have received — why not repeat it regularly? But this none of you will do. Follow your guru's instructions. How many of you do it? At most you sit a half an hour, tell the beads as if it were a drudgery, then get up and walk away. This won't help."

(Swami Saradananda, in Glimpses of a Great Soul)

Fragmented Mind and Focused Mind

"The mind has a natural proclivity towards the low and the vulgar, towards lust and lucre and towards name and fame. The task of the aspirant is to gather together the scattered mind and fix it on the lotus feet of the Lord. The highest ambition in life should be the realization of God."

(Swami Sivananda, For Seekers of God)

Living in the Eternal Moment

"Do not look backward during the tiresome journey through all the different stages of evolution, but always look forward to attain the highest point of spiritual development. Then, if you want to know your past lives you will recollect them. Nothing will remain unknown to you. Time and space will vanish, and past and future will be transformed into the eternal present."

(Swami Abhedananda, in Reincarnation)

SCRIPTURAL SAYINGS
of the World's Religious Traditions

"Knowing the corporeal body to be as fragile as an old earthen jar, the arhat fortifies the mind and makes it like a citadel. Then he settles in, sharpens his wisdom sword, and battles with mara. With every victory, he protects what he has gained, but free of attachment."

"The Supreme Deity is without beginning or end. It brings about the world, then hides Itself amidst chaos there. All the forms present there are both manifested by It, and enveloped by It as well. If you come to know that transcendent and incomparable Entity, Who is one without a second, as your Divine Self, you will break free of all bonds."

"Dear soul: If thou hearkenest to the teacher and apply yourself to the teachings by applying your mind, thou shalt receive wisdom. Thus, lend thy ear to the subtleties that the wise instruct you in. Happy, indeed, is that one who nourishes himself on the words of the wise and learned, and shuts them up in his heart, well-guarded. That one will always be one of the wise."

"My son: Give me thy heart and let my light shine through you. Allow thine eyes to see and serve my ways. Do no evil and evil shall not come unto thee. Stay far away from the unjust, and sin will remain far away from thee."

"So long as you are not dead to all things transitory and substanceless, you will not be able to enter into that highest Portico. Otherwise, when you finally come into that most sacred Place, you shall find, to your awe, only One sole Being replacing the world and all its living creatures."

"Each thing in the cosmos shoots forth, then flowers, only to return to its roots again. All of this is in perfect conformity with nature. Therefore, the destruction and death of the body poses no danger to the soul."

ALEXANDER HIXON

AN INTERVIEW WITH DUDJOM RINPOCHE

The reason why western therapy does not work to produce Enlightenment is due to its lack of taking refuge in a higher power. Just leaving the mind to its own devices only reveals emptiness, which is the void behind the mind and its thoughts. There is no "safe space" within the mind to go to; that is a fable. The only safe space lies beneath the mind as its substratum. Religious tradition says, take refuge there, and experience fullness, called mature emptiness.

Lex Hixon: Your Holiness: When you were giving the public talk recently, you sat very silently, and everyone in the audience was sitting silently with you. And there was a sense of not just quietness, but some kind of power in the atmosphere. Can you somehow explain to us what you were doing at that time?
Dudjom Rinpoche (through translator): He says he did not do any special thing. But as we find in the teachings, in the precise way we are taught, in the way we do the practice and meditation, we have to separate the positive and the negative thoughts. Then, very gradually, there comes this deeper silence.
Lex Hixon: How does one go about separating the positive and negative thoughts in the beginning, and how are they to b known to be different?
Dudjom Rinpoche: In the beginning, most beings do not separate the two. And so, the teachings tell us to become aware of the "black" thoughts. These arise from the negative emotions, such as attachment, and anger, and ignorance. These thoughts create the illusory root of samsara. So we practice distinguishing the positive and the negative thoughts, or white and black thoughts. Thoughts that are free of attachment, hatred, and ignorance help us generate qualities such as devotion and compassion. Thus, in the beginning, to help towards complete purification of mind, we carefully tend to our good and bad thoughts in this purely dharmic way.
Lex Hixon: Is it possible to tame those thoughts without engaging in religious practice? Tibetan Buddhism is a religion with many practices and many forms of training, and people living in this country today may feel that they can train their thoughts directly without any kind of special religious practices. Is this possible?
Dudjom Rinpoche: In the West, it seems to us that people do go through the first phase of the practice — that of watching their thoughts. But without going through the full process and affirming that negative thoughts and positive thoughts are well separated, followed by the empty mind getting studied in meditation, all results will be empty and devoid of any real meaning in the end.
Lex Hixon: Pardon me, but for even further clarification, a Western psychologist might say, that watching the thoughts as being both negative and positive and coming to a final conclusion would be possible without taking any religious practices and without taking refuge in any tradition. So how would the Rinpoche explain to the Western psychologist his point of view?
Dudjom Rinpoche: In the teachings of Tibet, in the beginning, we are always keeping the focus upon the two noble truths at the rel-

ative level, so as to purify the thoughts after the separation process has been accomplished. In this way, the mind does not merely return to thinking an admixture of good and bad thoughts, as most people in the world do, including here in the West. One does not separate for the sake of distinction and then go back to thinking along dual lines. To purify the mind is a further goal.
Lex Hixon: Forgive me for asking for further clarification, but many Western psychologists do not have the kind of powers and energies that the dharma and religious traditions can put at their disposal, therefore they are trying to work on the mind with the mind, but without these dharma powers and insights — like refuge in the Three Jewels and the refuge in the blessed Lama.
Dudjom Rinpoche: According to the Buddha dharma that we follow, in order to attain the nature of mind which is totally shunyata, emptiness, is that first we have to get support of what is called the entrance, or first part of the practice, which is virtue, etc. This is because we have to purify or perfect the different perceptions, like about samsara and nirvana both together. Otherwise just saying that everything is empty, or just thinking about virtue and non-virtue, will only lead to nihilism, like here in the West, i.e., just thinking about some kind of concept instead of gaining higher realization. It would end up as obscured emptiness rather than realization of Emptiness. Therefore we combine the practice of relative and absolute truth with compassion; it all goes together.
Lex Hixon: So the mind somehow has to be purified in order for it to see itself directly? Is that what you are suggesting?
Dudjom Rinpoche: Yes, we have to purify our deluded perceptions with the basic or common practices before entering into the intermediate and advanced levels. Refuge in Buddha will set the stage and lead to advancement free of false starts; then we can reach inward to the higher practices even more successfully.
Lex Hixon: The interesting thing about Buddhist practices is that the highest mysticism, what you call the highest teachings, is known to the practitioner from the beginning, even though he or she must begin with the relative teachings. Can the beginner, as the early practices begin, be aware that the mind is pure by its very nature, and that all thoughts are exactly of the same essence?
Dudjom Rinpoche: All beings have the intrinsic nature of the Buddha; we all have the essence of Enlightenment. Yet along the way, the path gets obscured. We need to purify these perceptions with a general practice and a particular practice, which is to recog-

nize the nature of the self as emptiness; combining the relative and the absolute will accomplish this. A bird cannot fly with one wing. The relative and absolute are these very two wings that allow the practitioner to ascend to higher and higher levels of realization.
Lex Hixon: And they can be carried on at the same time? The relative does not have to come first, and then the absolute later?
Dudjom Rinpoche: It is important to combine the practice together. When we do the general practice, such as taking refuge, conjoined with the absolute, there is a special purity that comes, and grows when we do prostrations and refuge prayers. All these combined become one refuge and will give the man realization of his nature. These relative merits of practice have to combine with the truth of the absolute to lead to the understanding of the nature of mind as being empty. Without these, realization of emptiness would not lead that far, as is seen with ordinary people. Without this combined endeavor at the very outset, the effect will be an immature emptiness that only contributes to completely obscuring oneself, just like it always does along the materialistic path.
Lex Hixon: To be convinced of the true nature of the mind, it seems that the only way that we can, is by meeting someone in whom the mind is purified. And I felt that, the other evening, when his holiness was sitting quietly with everyone, that all of us, to s small degree, got a glimpse of the intrinsic purity and peace of the mind. So, I was wondering if his holiness could tell us how he became convinced of the purity of mind through the deep contact with an illumined teacher, and what was that teacher like?
Dudjom Rinpoche: Of course, meeting the teacher is important. Without that we would not receive instructions, and without those we would not be able to perform practice free of errors, and then do meditation leading to accomplishment and realization. His holiness, himself, did not do many practices, since from the beginning he was always doing dharma activities. He was always giving out special profound teachings that can really lead one to realization, to attain total enlightenment while here in the body. For most, practice is very important, however, so that one can make progress via better connections in future lives. With total concentration combined with higher teachings, one can attain to enlightenment of the rainbow body in 7 years, sometimes in less. So practice after gaining instructions is highly enjoined on the practitioner, as it is and always has been in all authentic spiritual pathways.
Lex Hixon: Does his holiness feel that there are people here in the West who actually have the highest goal in mind, or does he feel that here in this country they are, at most, just making those good connections for the greater benefit of their future lifetimes?
Dudjom Rinpoche: That is difficult to say, but whoever has exposure to this dharma, even if they just have sincere interest, and have positive thoughts of joy and happiness for others that he would give them the teachings, give them personal instructions, and seeing that their good connections from past lives come forward at that time, they would make swift progress in the dharma. The difficulty is, when the child is born here, they are just given a name, and not the dharma instructions, so they have little chance of remembering their past connections. If his holiness can give them the spiritual name, later, after they come and approach him, then everything then depends upon their practice after that.
Lex Hixon: You mentioned the blessing of Vajradhara. Can you

> *"These relative merits of practice have to combine with the truth of the absolute to lead to the understanding of the nature of mind as being empty. Without these, realization of emptiness would not lead that far, as is seen with ordinary people. Without this combined endeavor at the very outset, the effect will be an immature emptiness that only contributes to completely obscuring oneself, like it does along the materialistic path."*

explain the nature of who or what Vajradhara is? This might be a surprise to some psychologists who do not know that such a thing as Vajradhara exists to help them realize th nature of mind.
Dudjom Rinpoche: As we have the intrinsic nature within us of the Buddha himself, through the practice of absorption, this ordinary mind can dissolve into total voidness, devoid of particles of doubt. And with further practice of primordial purity, and the practice of spontaneity which leads beyond, then the body will manifest as light. This happens only through the practice of absorption. These are very profound and exalted teachings. To attain this level of highest realization entirely depends upon the teachings of Dzogchen, brought to Tibet by its two main teachers.
Lex Hixon: Rinpoche, why would one want their body to just disappear into light, or into rainbows, in the first place?
Dudjom Rinpoche: This body, called gross body, is the result of karma that has obscured our wisdom, and through the power of practice, and meditation, this delusional body can dissolve into the subtle body. Even if we could not dissolve into the rainbow body, we can practice awakening the potential of the subtle body to things like nadis, prana, and bindus — perfecting and purifying all this into pure perceptions like manifesting everything as the mandalas and different deities — then all appearances will manifest as the deities and the sounds of the mantras, and the display of all thought as the dharmata nature. Since we have not dissolved this physical body yet, and therefore remain ignorantly attached in this body, there are these many obstructions — like mining rocks, crushing stones, climbing mountains, enjoying objects, going into space, etc., which only continue to distract us away from attaining this, peaceful, blissful, inner light body, or the pure mind.
Lex Hixon: So is it possible that a person who has had this highest realization, yet who is still living, that they might appear to have a physical body which functions in the ordinary way, but that all the nervous system has been completely purified by these practices — that this very body is really not an ordinary body at all?
Dudjom Rinpoche: Even though these beings, through internal practices, have purified the nadis, prana, and bindus, and every-

thing into purity, yet they remain as if ordinary. Even if certain souls reach to the third stage of absorption, which is beyond practices, yet, in order to benefit other beings, they would remain in the physical form and give out the teachings of Mahayana Buddhism. These souls who are not the physical body, yet, penetrate through that body so that others can see their form, hear their speech, be close to their bodies, touch their bodies, and in that way benefit all beings at the ordinary level. There are already many beings here who have reached into recognition our their true Buddha nature, who have attained the awareness stage, and when reaching that level, get into the fourth stage, and have the full vision of the Buddha Nature, and who have then finished their practice stage, yet remain and do not dissolve into the rainbow body in order to help other beings. They can attain the great kingdom of dharmakaya, yet in order to benefit all sentient beings, do through very good karmas, they could very definitely liberate you.
Lex Hixon: So given the fact that these beings are so powerful, we do not then have to worry about not having enough of these realized beings on the whole planet. Is this not so, your Holiness?
Dudjom Rinpoche: At that very moment, with that very being, they will indeed, even if there was only one of them, attend to the growth of others according to the karmas of each being. It would be difficult, however, to benefit all the beings of the world at once, but some of these more inwardly powerful ones can do so to a whole culture, or even to an entire country, even if only generally.
Lex Hixon: Your holiness: will you please pray for all of us through Vajradhara, make a great wish for us, and bless all of us who are listening, that we can realize now that all of our ordinary bodies and minds are really that divine essence of the pure gold of the rainbow body?

> " ....through the power of their realization and compassion, they benefit others in a unique way. They have, through their inspiration and wish, the ability to benefit all living beings. They have been empowered to benefit others by the great beings beyond and behind them. Whatever wish they make, what boon they confer, will manifest. They benefit through all kinds of ways, unseen to others. One would not believe, even to see this. If you garner close connection to them, they can even completely liberate you."

not pass from their body into the rainbow body. Even if these beings decide to keep their physical bodies for this purpose, they possess an internal protection that keeps them safe from illnesses, epidemics, etc. Similarly, their are many Dzogchen masters, and yogis, who when they leave their physical bodies, keep that body for future births on earth, and do not completely transform themselves into the rainbow body. It is most difficult to understand, and impossible to judge. It depends entirely on the individual concerning this immersion into the rainbow light body.
Lex Hixon: So, in a being of this high attainment, everything about them, including the physical, and all the words they say, have some sort of tremendous power. Is it a power that can further purify? Is it kind of like a burning heat that can melt, as it were, the as of yet still crystalized bodies of other practitioners?
Dudjom Rinpoche: Yes, through the power of their realization, and their compassion, and the ability of force that they gain through this realization, they can benefit others in a unique way.

And not only that, they have, through their inspiration and wish, the ability to benefit living beings. Also, they have been empowered to benefit others by the great beings beyond and behind them. Whatever wish they make, what boon they confer, will manifest. They benefit through all kinds of ways, unseen to others. One would not believe, even to see thi. If you garner close connection to them

Dudjom Rinpoche: (Offers the prayer in Tibetan): We should all realize now, due to that prayer, that whoever has a connection with such a guru, that this connection signifies the last birth in this universe. We can now attend upon the primordial Buddha at the Vajradhara level. And if we cannot reach that level after practices we undertake for purification, yet, then whoever has a connection through such prayers and wishes, that we will be able to move into the Buddha fields with our guru. Once we get there, and see Guru Padmasambhava, then he will give us whatever we need. We all should think unanimously in wishing this upon everyone.
Lex Hixon: Somehow, the words that you have spoken here today, and have poured into us, will turn us all into pure gold, and hopefully we will be able to illuminate our lives with them. Your Holiness, my final question is, will most of us complete our necessary spiritual practices there in the inner realm, or here?
Dudjom Rinpoche: Those who pray, and wish to have enlightenment, after death, when they go to the intermediate bardo, and if they have the definite experience of light, then they will be able to gain realization there. Some of those may come back to benefit others and assist them in reaching that deep experience, but it is really indefinite, and hard to tell with so many different individuals.

◆ ANNAPURNA SARADA

WHEN "THE GREAT SWAMI" WAS AMONG US
The Significance of Swami Vivekananda Today

Narendra was perfect from his very birth. He is devoted to the ideal of the formless God. He is free from ignorance and delusion. He has no bonds. He is a great soul. He has many sterling qualities. He is an expert musician, both as a singer and a player, and he is a versatile scholar. He keeps his passions closely under control."
Sri Ramakrishna Paramahamsa

"*Death has come to my bedside; I have been through enough of work and play; let the world realize what contribution I have made; it will take quite a long time to understand that.*" - *Swami Saradananda, quoting Swami Vivekananda during his last days. (New Discoveries, 4: 521)*

Nearly 130 years ago, Swami Vivekananda astounded the educated American public with the bold teachings of Vedanta. Although, it is too short a time to assess all that his contribution has been, for it is still working itself out, the aim of this article is to take a journey into the past and look to the future by addressing the present.

Who were we as a people when he walked amongst us and introduced the Truth of Advaita, Nondual Reality, as the ultimate truth of existence, with the fire of revelation, and who are we today? Will we continue to unwrap the spiritual knowledge he lavished upon us? Will we lose the thread of connection and momentum? Vivekananda never "cared a whit" for name and fame. He said he was merely a "voice without a form." Yet, it is always wise to remember the Great Teachers of humanity and not lose our connection with Them. We do this by nurturing their message via spiritual practices in ourselves, our families, and our communities. We see the effects of losing that connection in the conventional masses of humanity, restless in heart and mind, anxious, depressed, selfish, greedy, violent and jealous, dominating or alienated – all lost in the search for happiness in things that can never give lasting peace or fulfillment, or deprived of the wherewithal for material happiness to begin with.

Swami Vivekananda arrived in the U.S. in 1893, and despite what some younger readers might think, this was not so long ago. The seeds of everything we take for granted today and foresee ahead, were sprouting in the great ferment of American and Western culture in the form of science, technology, and the arising of alternative religious movements. A featured and popular speaker at the Parliament of Religions at the Chicago World's Fair of 1893, the swami saw all the scientific and technological advances of the day on display. Vivekananda was a man of realization, *samadhi*, having the ability to concentrate at will on any given aspect of life and thought, able to trace its origin and its potential

Swami Vivekananda

futures. Such yogic abilities he used not for any selfish purpose but to help guide Eastern and Western civilizations onto a course where people could awaken to their identity as Atman, the ever-pure, eternal, indivisible Self/Soul temporarily housed in a body-mind complex. In this realization we would find all fulfillment, strength and fearlessness, as well as Love, Freedom, and so importantly, our Oneness with everything. "*This grand preaching, the oneness of things, making us one with everything that exists, is the great lesson to learn, for most of us are very glad to be made one with higher beings, but nobody wants to be made one with lower beings.*" For, global civilization was in its infancy; we were entering an era that required us to wake up from our dreams of separation and antagonism – in religion, among nations, among cultures, and individuals, if this current world was to continue.

"*I quite agree with you that only the Advaita philosophy can save mankind, whether in East or West, from 'devil worship' and kindred superstitions, giving tone and strength to the very nature of man. India herself requires this, quite as much or even more than the West. Yet it is hard uphill work, for we have first to create a taste, then teach, and lastly proceed to build up the whole fabric. Perfect sincerity, holiness, gigantic intellect, and an all-conquering will. Let only a handful of men work with these, and the whole world will be revolutionized. ... It is the patient upbuilding of character, the intense struggle to realize the truth, which alone will tell in the future of humanity.*" (Letter to Mr. Sturdy of England in 1895)

"*You will be struck dumb to find your presence everywhere in the world of soul and matter. You will feel the whole sentient and insentient world as your own self. Then you can't help treating all with the same kindness as you show towards yourself. This is indeed practical Vedanta. Do you understand me? Brahman is one, but is at the same time appearing to us as many, on the relative plane.*" (Talks with Swami Vivekananda)

Who Were We Back Then?

The Parliament of Religions rocketed Swami to the very fame he did not seek, but also opened the doors to the intellectual elite of Chicago, New York, Boston, and other places. He drew crowds

> "....the true goal of human existence can never be pleasure (rotating with pain) but realization of ourselves as Absolute Existence – beyond the reach of pleasure and sorrow, and one with Reality."

wherever he went, while making his way through the U.S. via several lecture bureaus. He later abandoned that work as he developed life-long friendships and students who wanted to see Vedanta spread. His friends and students were counted among university professors, open-minded clergy, aspiring and unconventional youth, the leaders of the new metaphysical movements, and educated, cultured men and women prominent in society.

Swamiji encountered a wonderful openness to new things in Americans, and with regard to spirituality, a hunger for Eastern teachings that proclaimed the ever-perfect nature of the Soul and its unity with all, which did not crumble *"by the terrible onslaughts of modern science."* The Americans he met, by and large, were either young, unmarried persons exhibiting a social and religious morality of chastity before marriage, or were married, both of whom engaged in charitable works, civic service, and disciplined conduct according to the rules of the day. They were friendly and worldly-wise.

However, he noted many times that most Americans by far were materialistic and liable to turn the teachings of Vedanta and Yoga back toward an expectation for physical results. Raised on either miracles or scientific skepticism, Swamiji had to introduce Vedanta in a way that led Americans inward with purity and a longing for spiritual emancipation and pure love for God, rather than mystery mongering. Back then, the new teachings from the East propagated by nascent "New Age" groups proclaiming our inherent perfection were more often than not measured by one's ability to heal disease, generate wealth or abundance, and attain desires in the world. Immature ideas concerning the afterlife had spawned seances by both the naively curious and charlatan entrepreneurs. Other metaphysical teachings were circulating, none based on a sound philosophical or cosmological footing, but even worse, they were not oriented toward Self-Realization, but to far lesser goals, thinking them high. Writing to an English friend and serious student of Indian Philosophy, the swami stated, *"....although some truth underlies the mass of mystical thought which has burst upon the Western world of late, it is for the most part full of motives, unworthy, or insane."*

Some of What Swamiji Taught Us

As a civilization, Americans were firmly entrenched in taking the body as the Self, i.e., "I am the body." Some religious sects believed in the restoration of the physical body in heaven (and still do); others, under the influence of science, did not believe in a soul, but only matter. Both views thereby take the body as the soul/self and the soul/self to be the body. That being the case, there naturally followed the ceaseless search for wealth, beauty, fame, and health, with pleasures and diversions of all kinds as the goal of life. Exceptions naturally existed.

As an example of this materialistic trend, many whom he met expected an ever increasing good, a heaven on earth, either through the practice of religious or metaphysical teachings, social virtues, or scientific discoveries. To counter these ideas, Vivekananda would state, "A good world is like saying hot ice." Going on, he would explain, this cannot be had in this world, pointing out the obvious: while feeding one part of the planet, another part starves; while eliminating one disease another springs up; and, where every rise is followed by a fall, every pleasure with its opposite; death after life, etc. Instead, he held out the practical truth of Vedanta: if we do not want the bad, we must give up the good, for they are forever linked like the poles of a magnet; they are *"a difference in manifestation, not of kind."*

Americans heard for the first time: there is the Absolute Existence, attained in what the swami referred to as the Superconscious state, and there is the relative existence, our common psycho-physical experiences. The former is our true Self, whose unlimited Freedom and Bliss we are seeking externally. It is Existence, Knowledge, and Bliss absolute. Relativity, on the other hand, is the veil of limited, individual existence and the myriad objects appearing to us due to the presence of time, space, causation, names, and forms. Everything in relativity rises and falls, appears and dissolves, rotating on the wheels of good/bad, happiness/sorrow, life/death. Thus, the true goal of human existence can never be pleasure (rotating with pain) but realization of ourselves as Absolute Existence – beyond the reach of pleasure and sorrow, and one with Reality. In one of his lectures, Vivekananda stated, *"Sense-happiness is not the goal of humanity. Wisdom (Jnâna) is the goal of all life. We find that man enjoys his intellect more than an animal enjoys its senses; and we see that man enjoys his spiritual nature even more than his rational nature. So, the highest wisdom must be this spiritual knowledge. With this knowledge will come bliss. All these things of this world are but the shadows, the manifestations in the third or fourth degree of the real Knowledge and Bliss."* Complete Works (CW) vol. 3 p. 1

Detaching from relativity, i.e. giving up both bad and good, the seeking of pleasure and shunning of pain, is the practical conclusion. Yet, the subtlety of this renunciation in our society, was, and continues to be, difficult to grasp, being far different than merely rejecting objects, but rather seeing the Eternal in the noneternal, and thus taking one's stand on that Eternal, Absolute Reality rather than in matter, inclusive of body or mind. *"The American people are too young to understand renunciation." "It will take a long time for the Westerners to understand the higher spirituality. Everything is [money] to them. If a religion brings them money or health or beauty or long life, they will all flock to it, otherwise not."* CW vol.5 p.221; Letters, p. 137

Thus, it was not surprising, that despite the ability of many to grasp the philosophical teachings of *Advaita*, there was still a habitual trend of mind to compromise and justify these teachings via life in the body. The *Advaita* of which he taught was based on the true nature of the Soul as transcendent of not just the body, but also of

> "It is not possible to simply jump from the floor of taking matter to be real to the rooftop of nondual understanding. Qualification for understanding Vedanta relies on the "stairs" of Yogic practice, and the upper limbs of Yoga are based on the cosmology of the Sankhya System. This cosmology takes into account not only the physical universe, but proposes/explains the subtle causes for it, and those subtle causes are the effects of even more subtle causes, until one is traversing inwardly from physical matter, to energy, thought, Intelligence, and Cosmic Mind."

thoughts, emotions, mind, intellect, and individual ego. This tendency (*samskara*) to cling to the physical appearances of this world would also lead to a misunderstanding of the *Vedanta*, and *Yoga*, which he also brought, causing a detour from the aim of true Religion and spirituality.

"The Vedanta preaches the ideal; and the ideal, as we know, is always far ahead of the real, of the practical, as we may call it. There are two tendencies in human nature: one to harmonize the ideal with the life, and the other to elevate the life to the ideal. It is a great thing to understand this, for the former tendency is the temptation of our lives. I think that I can only do a certain class of work. Most of it, perhaps, is bad; most of it, perhaps, has a motive power of passion behind it, anger, or greed, or selfishness. Now if any man comes to preach to me a certain ideal, the first step towards which is to give up selfishness, to give up self-enjoyment, I think that is impractical. But when a man brings an ideal which can be reconciled with my selfishness, I am glad at once and jump at it. That is the ideal for me." CW vol. 2 p.293

"To put the Hindu ideas into English and then make out of dry philosophy and intricate mythology and queer startling psychology, a religion which shall be easy, simple, popular, and at the same time meet the requirements of the highest minds – is a task only those can understand who have attempted it. The dry, abstract Advaita must become living – poetic – in everyday life; out of hopelessly intricate mythology must come concrete moral forms; and out of bewildering Yogi-ism must come the most scientific and practical psychology – and all this must be put in a form so that a child may grasp it. That is my life's work. The Lord only knows how far I shall succeed. 'To work we have the right, not to the fruits thereof.'" Letters, p. 284

As Swamiji became more and more familiar with the American view of reality and its collective tendencies, one of the issues he noted is that we were missing a cosmology. *Vedanta*, *Yoga*, *Sankhya* - three Indian systems which he brought under the general heading of *Vedanta* - are all systems of turning the senses, mind, and intellect inward to uncover the true Self/Soul. (See Nectar #36, "The Triple Gem of Vedanta") If the religious public of America at that time had any way of turning inward, or at least setting the world aside to find God, it was through devotion to Jesus or the Almighty Father. Yet, the lack of a perceived coherent and practical philosophy in the common Christian traditions, and in the face of scientific reason, was driving away wisdom-seeking intellectuals. Meanwhile, the more universally-minded faithful, sympathetic to ideas of oneness with all, were leaning toward mystical and Eastern thought, which are nondogmatic and based on direct spiritual experience open to all.

Thus, how were we to gain direct experience of the Atman/Absolute Existence? It is not possible to simply jump from the floor of taking matter to be real to the rooftop of nondual understanding. Qualification for understanding *Vedanta* relies on the "stairs" of Yogic practice, and the upper limbs of *Yoga* are based on the cosmology of the *Sankhya System*. This cosmology takes into account not only the physical universe, but proposes/explains the subtle causes for it, and those subtle causes are the effects of even more subtle causes, until one is traversing inwardly from physical matter, to energy, thought, Intelligence, and Cosmic Mind. Turning within is aided immensely by knowing the inner terrain and its forces. In this way we needed some understanding of Eastern cosmology to lead us inward.

Swamiji saw that we did not know about akasha and prana, and thus how the universe is projected and withdrawn in cycles. Knowledge of these two facilitates control of senses, mind, and its thoughts, helps us recognize the presence of karma and samskaras affecting our thoughts, desires, and actions, all leading to an understanding of how reincarnation operates. With knowledge of these we can solve our questions about life and existence and rise above the bondage of identification with matter, gross and subtle. We may say, "I am not the body," "I am not the mind and its thoughts," but if that only gives us a cozy feeling of relief, and not the ability to be a detached, unaffected witness of the joys and sorrows of life, fearless in the face of the body's death, what to speak of losing a job or a loved one, then it is nothing but parroting an affirmation. In his lecture on "The Vedanta Philosophy," Vivekananda gave us a concise version of Indian cosmology:

"The belief about cycles is as follows: All matter throughout the universe is the outcome of one primal matter called Âkâsha; and all force, whether gravitation, attraction or repulsion, or life, is the outcome of one primal force called Prâna. Prana acting on Akasha is creating or projecting the universe. At the beginning of a cycle, Akasha is motionless, unmanifested. Then Prana begins to act, more and more, creating grosser and grosser forms out of Akasha – plants, animals, men, stars, and so on. After an incalculable time this evolution ceases and involution begins, everything being resolved back through finer and finer forms into the original Akasha and Prana, when a new cycle follows. Now there is something beyond Akasha and Prana. Both can be resolved into a third thing called Mahat – the Cosmic Mind. This Cosmic Mind does not create Akasha and Prana, but changes itself into them." Complete Works vol. 1 p. 351

It is also interesting to know from a historical perspective, that Nikola Tesla was fascinated by Swamiji's presentation of *akasha* and *prana*, as Vivekananda wrote to a friend: *"Mr. Tesla was charmed to hear about the Vedantic Prâna and Âkâsha and the Kalpas, which according to him are the only theories modern science can entertain. Now both Akasha and Prana again are produced from the cosmic Mahat, the Universal Mind, the Brahmā or Ishvara. Mr. Tesla thinks he can demonstrate mathematically that force and matter are reducible to potential energy. I am to go and see him next week, to get this new mathematical demonstration."* – Letters p. 281

We can note here for further clarification that all of this is happening in relativity, whether in the physical or heavenly realms, on up to the *Mahat*, Cosmic Mind. The *Atman-Brahman* is the one sentient, immutable Reality lending existence to all forms, gross and subtle, and filling them with consciousness according to their manifestation. This is *"the Eternal in noneternal,"* described in the Upanisads. Thus, knowledge of the cosmology grants the practitioner the ability to discriminate between the Self and the non-Self, become the Witness, and through spiritual practice (*sadhana*) and grace, realize their identity as *Atman-Brahman*.

With regard to *prana*, as lifeforce, it may have been familiar with some healers in American then, but not understood. In translations of Eastern spirituality that were making their way West, prana was translated as breath, which could not be well understood by those unfamiliar with Sanskrit and Eastern thought. In Vivekananda's lectures on *Raja Yoga* (the Yoga Sutras), the swami delineated not only prana as it pertains to its five-fold operations in the body, but also what he coined as "psychic prana," or the *prana* that moves our thoughts. This is a tremendous elucidation for those being introduced to Traditional *Yoga*, even today, who study these lectures and sutra commentaries; for the word "breath" in English does not convey the vast scope of the meaning of *prana*. Understanding these two aspects of *prana*, and gaining control of them, makes for the difference between remaining bound to the body and the experiences gained in it, and achieving concentration, meditation, and *samadhi* utilizing them.

All the above concerning what Swami Vivekananda taught us, is a bare "sound byte," intended only to pair up what our historical predilections were, and a few important teachings that if plumbed to their depth and practiced would address these issues and free us from bondage and the fear that comes from thinking we are limited creatures.

Another point Swamiji would often make about Americans as a collective is that the people of the day could not take in any large amounts of philosophy. Remember his quote above about the lengths he was striving to go to present an endlessly profound philosophy (used for millennia to attain Self-Realization) in a way that would be easy to understand. Truth may be simple to those who have realized It; for It is hiding in plain sight always. Recognizing It is another thing entirely, and further, takes preparation and qualification. Along with this handicap, however, was another more poignant critique, which continues to be experienced by authentic teachers and persevering students today. It is that we exhibited insufficient commitment to treading the path and

The Art Institute of Chicago, ca. 1893

instead would move on to the next new fad. He called us *"straw on fire."*

Who Are We Today?

The flow of change in our society is not in a straight line. We have had cycles of social/economic/cultural openness followed by constriction. Swamiji was here during a time of openness in a "society" that was apparently more homogenous and of European ancestry when it came to the educated masses. Since then, the U.S. has become far more diverse ethnically and religiously, and today, more polarized than we have been in many generations. In Swamiji's time, a man could support his family on his income, leaving married women free to attend classes and volunteer. Today,

> "Emotions and passions are driven by the unripe ego that swells with pride on one hand, and deflates with low self-esteem on the other, and many varieties in between. Dependence on "feelings" and "emotions" to lead one along the path skew one's perception of the teacher and teachings, resulting in exaggerated enthusiasm and humility often followed by the opposite and a quick departure from the path."

for the vast majority of people at least two full time incomes are required; many people have to work multiple jobs; Sunday is not a universal day of rest. In the 1800's Sri Ramakrishna stated that *"worldliness is the chronic disease of the age,"* and Swamiji certainly saw that this was true in the West as well. Today, they might both say that distraction coupled with worldliness is the chronic disease of our generations. Worldliness is the constant seeking of pleasure and enjoyment as the aim of life.

Vedanta and Buddhism were widely introduced through the Parliament of Religions in 1893. Since then, we have seen waves of various Indian traditions and lineages, the Tibetan, Zen, and Dzogchen streams of Buddhism, then Islam and Sufism, and a strong interest in Native American and indigenous religions, and others. And along with these have come ever-diversifying groups of New Age/New Thought and metaphysics, often hybridizing with Eastern and Middle Eastern teachings. Whereas Vedanta was the new option in contrast to Christianity and Judaism in the U.S. when Vivekananda was here, now, nearly every city of the country has "alternative religions" of some kind available.

But has this made us more spiritual, more illumined and liberated? There seem to be two opposing views: one, that there is a mass awakening to higher consciousness happening across the globe; versus, two, a sense that people are failing to take a spiritual path meant for Liberation i.e., Enlightenment, to its final consummation. Readers will have to draw their own conclusions.

Straw On Fire And Instant Clarification

Still, how often, we find, that seekers are stuck in endless menu-tasting. The internet has made it possible to sample anything – to watch all kinds of spiritual and religious teachers, to jump from one teaching and tradition to another without the benefit of background, authoritative, personal guidance, or the proper atmosphere, and probably interrupted by many distractions. The individualistic character of people born in the U.S. (of any ethnic background), has not prepared them to understand the necessity of a teacher. Internet culture enforces the idea that if we want to know something, we can just Google it. Any teacher will do. Any answer that appeals to us (i.e. our egos) will do. Only rarely, and more and more by chance, does a serious seeker find a qualified teacher, realize that they need to set everything else aside and take the teachings from that teacher/lineage to its depths. This is merely the continuation of Vivekananda's observation of the American "straw on fire" *samskara*; and serious aspirants have to overwrite this habit with perseverance and fidelity.

Operating in tandem with this is the expectation of instant gratification that has been ingrained in the U.S. for generations. People want quick results rather than to dedicate themselves to spiritual disciplines to purify the mind so that one's nature as the eternal Self is realized. This desire for instant illumination, or "sputnik samadhi," diffuses the spirit of commitment and enthusiasm that is needed in spiritual life, and leads people to seek for "an easier path."

Advaita Vedanta clearly expresses that there is one homogenous, all-pervasive Reality upon which all else is superimposed. Being a superimposition, the world of our mental-sensual experience is therefore unreal, having no existence of its own. This Reality alone is our Essence, our true nature, and nothing can ever take that away. When realized, it is obvious that no spiritual practice ever caused It to come into existence. It is never the effect of a cause, being ever present. This has led to the misleading statement that we do not need to do spiritual practice to gain It. The fact remains, however, that spiritual practice is necessary to qualify the mind to realize we have always and ever been that Reality. There are many nuances to how Grace and Self-effort go hand in hand. Those who warn beginning and intermediate aspirants that striving only holds Self-Realization away, are deluding them with half-truths and catering to this straw on fire/instant gratification handicap which must be overcome. Such teachings may fill their meeting centers or generate a huge following, but it will not lead to Self-Realization.

Emotionalism Vs. Manifestation

Today, as a culture, we are also far more emotional, and taken up with our emotions as well. Whether we suppressed it all in the 1800's or we were more mentally/emotionally balanced back then, this has become a big handicap for spiritual aspirants and spiritual circles. It is hard to find qualified seekers today who are free from emotional baggage of some kind. Emotions and passions are driven by the unripe ego that swells with pride on one hand, and deflates with low self-esteem on the other, and many varieties in

> "With this ancient knowledge and the Gita, we perceive more and more clearly that all action takes place in nature alone. This leads to growing fearlessness and Self-confidence, which allows us to face off with fears based in inadequacy and insecurity – for they are all based in the false idea that we are a body-mind complex only."

between. Dependence on "feelings" and "emotions" to lead one along the path skew one's perception of the teacher and teachings, resulting in exaggerated enthusiasm and humility often followed by the opposite and a quick departure from the path. It is not that Vedanta and Yogic practices cannot address emotions, but students need sufficient devotion to the Ideal, or a true and sincere longing to rise out of suffering to finally make headway. The Vedantic teachings around discrimination and detachment, *Viveka* and *Vairagya*, along with the six virtues of inner peace, self-control, etc., have led qualified spiritual aspirants along the path of Liberation for millennia. In the U.S., emotionalism and other issues present constant *karma*-laden distractions.

What, exactly, stands in our way? During a recent series of classes on how to successfully implement Advanced Spiritual Tools, Babaji Bob Kindler presented the following three groups of points as the obstacles and qualifications to gaining the full benefit of these essential practices.

One: Successful Purging of:
- Residual emotions from Upbringing
- Base attachments to possessions
- Possessiveness of people and objects
- Desire to control the lives of others
- Pride springing from egotism
- Fears based in inadequacy and insecurity

Two: Close Scrutiny of Matter in order to:
- Acknowledge that It cannot fulfill
- Comprehend that it is empty of substance
- Perceive that it consists of thought
- See that it is ever-changing
- Reveal that it is insentient

Three: Complete & Take Continuing Recourse to:
- Earning mantra-diksha & taking teachings from a qualified guru
- Practicing the first Five Limbs of Yoga*
- Contemplation of the Adhidaivavidya**
- Reading of the Gita & Upanisads
- Beginning and maintaining a daily meditation practice

* yama/beneficial denial, niyama/beneficial practices, asana/steady meditation posture, pranayama/control of physical and psychic lifeforce, pratyahara/ability to withdraw the senses and mind from objects

** 24 Cosmic Principles: 5 gross elements, 5 cognitive senses, 5 active senses, 5 subtle elements, 4 fold mind (manas, intellect, thought, I-sense), and also Cosmic Mind and/or unmanifested Prakriti – all of nature in potential/formless matter.

It should be noted, that each list benefits immensely by engaging the other two lists. In other words, we should seek to work on all three lists at once, best if in their presented order. This way emotions are matured into devotion, and passions associated with their objects are controlled by discriminative wisdom. The reasons for this are too numerous to cite, but here are a few:

By practice of the first limb of *Yoga* (consisting of nonviolence, truthfulness, non-stealing, moderation or chastity, and only taking what one needs) the emotional and passion-driven states arising from not observing them, along with additional *karmas* from bad actions, get neutralized and one ceases to create them anew. By studying the Bhagavad Gita, one comes to know that all actions proceeding from selfish desire generate *karma* and suffering. Via study of the Gita and Upanisads, one learns the glory of the Self and the emptiness of all finite things. All these must be contemplated under the guidance of the guru who is also there to answer questions and quell doubts. Further, the *Adhidaivavidya* is the science of cosmology, as we have already mentioned twice above. By contemplating it daily and understanding it with the help of the teacher and scriptures, one becomes intellectually convinced that the Self/Atman is distinct from all phenomena, and ever-free. With this ancient know-ledge and the Gita, we perceive more and more clearly that all action takes place in nature alone. This leads to growing fearlessness and Self-confidence, which allows us to face off with fears based in inadequacy and insecurity – for they are all based in the false idea that we are a body-mind complex only.

Taking Swami Vivekananda Into Our Future

While preparing for this article, the writer read anew Swami Vivekananda's Letters (Letters of Swami Vivekananda) and his conversations with disciples (Talks with Swamiji). What surfaced so strongly from this study and also from reflection on our country over the last 30 years of spiritual life and service, is that we have only begun to understand what the great Swami gave us, and we need to keep unwrapping his teachings in the context of the "nuts and bolts" of Indian Philosophy. Interestingly, there seems to be some consensus about this aided by the digital age, for we are seeing more and more Vedantic scripture, and Indian Philosophical systems taught in detail to householders, not just to monastics. During Swamiji's time here, he noted that Americans could handle only a little bit of philosophy – no large amounts. This continues to be true for most people. But we must remember that Vivekananda specifically brought Vedanta as the Yoga of Knowledge to us. As Sri Krishna states in the Bhagavad Gita, *"Knowledge is the Supreme Purifier."* Further, he presented the Vedanta in a universal, non-sectarian manner.

During Swami Vivekananda's time in the U.S., he saw our inherent worship of freedom, love, courage, service, liberty, and independence as American ideals. Drawing from the Vedanta, he

showed us the unlimited versions of each of these, how the *Advaita*, the nondual philosophy raises the limited forms to their culmination. Instead of freedom limited to political and social terms, he presented the absolute Freedom of the Soul, transcending matter, energy, thought, time, space, and causation. Instead of love conditioned by our attachments and aversions and limited to our families, communities, races, or religions, he taught of the timeless, unconditioned Love that reveals itself when we realize *"There is but One, the Knower, Self, without a name, without a form or stain, the Witness He appears as Nature, Soul, and thou art That!"* And, *"Say peace to all, from me no danger be to aught that lives. In those that dwell on high and those that lowly creep, I am the Self in all!"* Courage, based in death-defying brute force of will, is re-imagined and transformed through the knowledge that we are birthless and deathless Awareness/*Atman* and have always been so.

Swamiji addressed our Ideals via the Vedanta; he taught according to our noble aspirations and the necessary knowledge to take us to their culmination. As he says, we move from lower truth to higher truth, never from error to truth.

For Generations To Come

Yet, during his time here he did not or could not set before us exemplary role models from our own culture. He either had no time for this, or, more likely, there were none to hold up – American role models of perfect Freedom, free from the taint of politics and bigotry; persons of all-comprehending, unconditioned Love; American examples of spiritual Realization not limited by their own religious stream. Who, then, shall we hold up for our children here in America? Swami Aseshananda, during his Sunday lectures at the Portland Vedanta Society, would remind us that America has not yet produced a *Jivanmukta*, one Liberated in life. Who, then, are we to offer to our children as role models? will it be sports figures and billionaires? Scientists and politicians? Movie stars? Superheroes? If that is as high as we can go in offering our children and ourselves a role model, we will never produce a *Jivanmukta*.

I think that Swamiji left this for future generations to figure out, and I have some suggestions. Vivekananda, himself, should head the list of role models, first, because he came to the U.S. and spent years amongst us, and was himself our first in-person look at a *Jivanmukta*. Second, he was universal. He stood for universality – advaita/non-duality as the ultimate experience of all religions sincerely followed. Third, he represents all the American ideals cited above, and his entire life is full of such examples. Further, his life story is captivating and recent. Fourth, at a time when the U.S. is polarized by politics, economics, technology, race, culture, religion, and gender, he saw all beings as *"God walking on two legs,"* and gave us the philosophical tools to explain this high realization, and the methods to approach it experientially. The Atman, the true Soul of humanity transcends all such divisions, and we are That. But we must realize it, which takes perseverance and proper guidance. *"Advaita is the future religion of thinking humanity."* *"Mankind ought to be taught that religions are but the varied expressions of THE RELIGION, which is Oneness, so that each may choose that path that suits him best."*

Whatever religious tradition a child is born into, the parents should certainly uphold the saints, prophets, and bodhisattvas of that tradition and take great care to explain to their children why the virtues exemplified in those lives are worth emulating, as opposed to the cultural icons of today that only feed into the search for pleasure, fame, power, and wealth – all of which disappear in one lifetime and which produce suffering in the form of disease and mental anguish. The lives of saints and sages touch and benefit humanity forever. Still, Swami Vivekananda's life transcends sectarianism and exemplifies the love, compassion, renunciation, service, and mystic union all other religions hold up in various ways...and he walked amongst us.

Annapurna Sarada lives in Waimea, Hawai'i, where she serves as the President of SRV Associations and manages SRV publications. She also is the Associate Editor of Nectar of Nondual Truth.

"GODBLOGS," CONTINUED
"Brahman-Bytes" in the Aftermath of the Avatar's Descent

Extending the "godblogs" tradition in SRV, another set of symbolic stories from the Avatar of the Age are offered here, giving beings the opportunity to seek out realization of Divine Reality within them through a more readily accessible method — that of comprehending the meaning of all that is external. What appears in the realms of name and form, sometimes referred to as maya, is simply a reflection of that selfsame Reality. Both the trick of espying maya's covering power (avarana-shakti) and the mastery of seeing through maya in order to see all as Brahman, is accomplished by the practice of this attempt to see God in everything or, "practicing the presence" as it was once known as. For, as the Upanisads state, *"From the Infinite the finite has come, yet being infinite, only the Infinite remains."*

Straw on Fire, or Wet Wood
2 Undesirable Options: Burning Out & Catching Fire Too Slowly

One important remark that Swami Vivekananda made while he was present with us here on the physical plane was *"None of you have caught my fire."* The Americans, he said, are like *"straw on fire."* It other words, they are all very enthusiastic when they first hear of spirituality, but give up quickly when they find out that intense effort must be made to actually realize spiritual truths. In was in this accord that he stated that there are books by the thousands, temples by the hundreds, *"but oh, for an ounce of practice."*

The "burn out too swiftly" syndrome, when juxtaposed next to the "catch fire too slowly problem," leaves no viable option for spiritual advancement in mankind. This age characterizes such unfortunate retardation. Matter is empty, desires remain unfulfilled, hopes are always dashed, and satiation never comes, but the solution of solutions never gets discovered, which is to throw oneself wholeheartedly into sadhana, spiritual self-effort, until suffering is overcome and realization about the perfection of the human Soul dawns on the mind. Those who succeed here on earth first come to know The Goal of transcending the earth plane, then set the mind's refined concentration towards that end, brooking no substitutes along the way. Accepting lesser goals weakens the fabric of one's character over time. This ends in the "straw on fire" predicament. Such weakness also keeps the flames of aspiration from leaping up to consume the ever-accumulating ignorance of the mind caused by the "wet wood" obstacle. As the *Kaivalya Upanisad* puts it:

"That one who studies the Vedanta (Upanisads) gets purified by the Fires. This wisdom purifies the sins of taking intoxicants, indulging in mindless intercourse, violence and killing, and from all untoward deeds done, knowingly or unknowingly, in this lifetime. Those who seek the highest order of life study and repeat this every day. By practice of these truths, the ocean of samsara is dried up, and the fruit of Kaivalya is attained."

Om Peace, Peace, Peace!

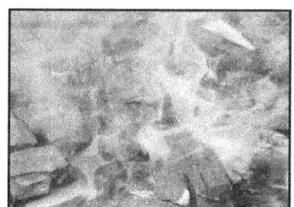

Spiritual Swimming Lessons
Breaking the Surface Requires a Teacher and Special Abilities

Sri Sarada Devi has advised that the people of this world read all the precious words that Sri Ramakrishna uttered in His lifetime — because *"They are all true."* Then, selecting those few that are most powerful and pertinent to the soul, each individual will need to *"....dive deep with them and realize Brahman."* In other words, one does not have to understand every little thing. How is that possible, anyway, since *Brahman* is infinite?

Somewhere amidst the many words that Thakur spoke to us in these times is mention of the difficulty of breaking the surface of the water so as to be able to reach deeper attainments. Some of us may remember our older brothers or sisters explaining to us how to

touch the bottom of the neighbor's swimming pool, whenever we were allowed into it. They also demonstrated this feat as we watched, in wonder. The entire matter is called "Tuck and Dive." To attempt to submerge the entire body as it lays flat, splashing about aimlessly on the surface, is not possible. And in truth, the fact that the body naturally floats, as they told us, is a confidence builder for the novitiate swimmer. And so the instructions went, grab your knees and turn the body into a ball, then taking a deep breath, dip the head under water and turn it towards the bottom of the pool. Then straighten out and apply the arms vigorously in order to break the surface. Once done, the body easily glides into deeper levels, and a new world of water sports opens up.

According to the Great Master, the ideal Paramahamsa, this is a good metaphor for piercing the surface of mayic appearances, as well. The beginning aspirant must, at some time, ball up the mental body against intrusions (like fear), tuck the head in the direction of the presence of *Brahman*, and exert the two strong arms of scriptural study and daily devotions to get free of gross and limiting worldly gravity and fathom the depths of formless meditation. As one famous song of Mother India expresses it:

*"Dive deep, oh mind,
dive deep into the ocean of God's beauty.
If you descend to the uttermost depths,
there you will find the gem of Love...."*

Man-unkind
Simpler to Destroy Than Create

As the Divine Mother, Sri Sarada Devi, observed mankind throughout Her life of selfless service, She rued the presence of hatred and ill will in so many living beings. Once, She exclaimed: *"It is so much easier to tear down than to build up."* She was speaking specifically of people's tendency to criticize others, and find fault with one another. Swami Vivekananda also joined in with this lament, saying, *"Oh, when will man be friend to man,"* and cited how the quality of jealousy was a bane upon his nation, and around the world.

So, the goal of human solidarity, support, and sympathy is still a ways off. The precepts of all of India's religious pathways, like Vedanta, Buddhism, and Jainism, begin with attaining and maintaining a non-aggressive nature. They proceed by inculcating non-coveting of the land, property, and goods of others. They mature under the auspice of maturing the emotions, mind, and intellect, then end with performing selfless service of other beings while seeing God in them. This is the way to live, and all those who will not "build up" in this way become the servants of all that is destructive and devilish. Even those who remain clear of violence, yet move to impede and undermine the good works of others, are still perpetrating violence, nevertheless. As Swami Vivekananda stated in this regard:

"How easily this world can be deluded by evil. What a mass of fraud has gathered over the devoted head of poor humanity since the dawn of civilization. There are people who are ready to pick holes in everything, but when it comes to the question of helpful work and selfless service, not a scent of them can be had. These people will go along the negative track until they are actually reduced to nothing! I pity them. It is not their fault. They are children, yay, veritable children, though they be great and high in society."

How Brahman is in Everything
Inseparable Despite Appearances, All-Pervasive Despite Seeming Divisions

There is a rare story that was told about Sri Ramakrishna, rather than by Sri Ramakrishna, and it is excellent for describing the homogenous nature of *Brahman*. When members of our SRV sangha were in Kolkata on one of its many pilgrimages, and visiting the Belur Math temple of the Ramakrishna

Order, Swami Damodaranandaji Maharaj met with us personally on several occasions and told us rare stories not readily found in the published books on Sri Ramakrishna.

One of these stories had to do with the Great Master sitting early one morning, just prior to sunrise, with one of His close-in disciples. The scene before them was beautiful, as the sun came over the horizon and began to light up all the objects of nature and culture around them, on all sides. Inspired by the peace and depth of the moment, the disciple ventured a question, saying, "Revered Sir: How is it that Brahman can be present in all beings? I do not understand how this can be possible." Drawing the disciple's attention to the now sparkling temple grounds in front of them, Thakur pointed and exclaimed, *"Just as you see the numerous dew drops before you all reflecting the light of the one Sun in the sky, so too do the forms of human beings reflect the Light of the One Brahman."* There was hardly anything more to say, or any further commentary needed. The disciple fell into deep reverie, the Master, into Samadhi.

How beautiful these words, and how simple yet explanatory. In this way is Truth and Its expression simple if one is observant and sensitive to It. There was one instance, similar to the dewdrop analogy, that took place recently, when marchers for World Peace lit candles one particular night and stood together in a crowd. This occurred in several countries around the world, simultaneously. If one looked at the spectacle from the ground one could see people with many candles, but from the air, looking from a helicopter, the scene looked like one ocean of light.

The higher view, then, from higher mind, availing oneself of the detached witness position is most favorable, and will allow the individual to perceive the truth of Oneness. With lower mind in control, the imposition of variety covers the Truth, and questions unending, void of conclusive answers, becomes the norm. As Hastamalaka has stated, in his stotram:

"It is one homogenous presence that causes all eyes to see. It is one omniscient entity which graces all minds with thought. It is like unto the sun which reveals the world of name and form for perceiving. That One and I are non-distinct and form one cohesive unity."

*— For more Godblogs
go to
community.srvwisdom.org*

Swami Sunirmalananda

TWO ASPECTS OF REALITY
The Roles and Distinctions of Vedanta and Advaita

Vedanta has attracted the attention of the world recently. However, Vedanta is sometimes confused with *Advaita*, and Advaita is often confused with some sort of magic called *maya*. Thus, "everything is nothing" becomes sort of a tranquilizer, and people imagine that someday everything vanishes and they only shall be left. Advaita is then misunderstood as our lives being lived in a non-existent illusory simulation called the universe, which covers *Brahman*.

Before Swami Vivekananda came, there lived in the Himalayan regions numerous sadhus. There is a tiny story concerning one of them. Once, a monk fell ill. A few others around him said, *"Jagat trikal me nahi hai,"* meaning, "this world is non-existent in all the three phases of time." Saying this, they left that ill monk to his fate. The unreality of the world, as understood by budding *Advaitins*, causes not a little concern. Brooding too much on the unreality of the world rather than the Reality Itself is perhaps the greater problem here. If there is this unreal world, there should be a base on which it stands. If the universe is unreal, you and I, all so-called persons, are also unreal. While the Buddhists deny a permanent basis or foundation behind the appearance, Vedanta stresses that foundation. And that base is Reality. That Reality is called Brahman. Brahman is not "god." Neither is maya just a blanket covering Reality, or Brahman, so that you and I can pull the blanket off to see Brahman. It's not as easy as all that.

said that your ego, the false perception of being an individual, is untrue. There is only one Reality, and that is Brahman. About this Brahman, we shall discuss now.

So What is all This About Vedanta?

Vedanta is not about Advaita alone. Most of us are aware of this truth. Advaita is the highest way of looking at Reality and its manifestations. Why so? The reason is, Advaita is not-two. Where there are two things, there is incompleteness. Oneness brings completion, fullness. At the ultimate state there is fullness. So Advaita is considered the ultimate way of understanding the truth. We all should attain to this Advaitic state of consciousness, we are advised, where duality, which creates disharmony, is eliminated. That still state of Oneness is our Ideal State of being, as we are That. And that state is the goal of all life.

The central theme of Vedanta, especially of one of its branches, Advaita Vedanta, is Brahman. Brahman means "expansive." or "vast." It is Limitlessness. The other etymological meaning of the term is "to expand." It is That out of which everything comes, as it were. This is the idea.

As was said, Brahman is not "god," but is the basis, the foundation, the core of everything. When we speak of Brahman as limitless, we remove all conditioning, all ideas of Brahman's having some form, all notions of duality, etc. That is, the Infinite is

> "Advaita is the highest way of looking at Reality and its manifestations. Why so? The reason is, Advaita is not-two. Where there are two things, there is incompleteness still. Oneness brings completion, fullness. At the ultimate state there is fullness. So Advaita is considered the ultimate way of understanding the truth."

Advaita, therefore, says that there is only One Reality. Nothing else. Not even you and I. Everything else is superimposition in time. There is one more way of putting the same thing: what we call "universe" is purely name, form, and time. In space-time, there is this universe of name and form. This *nama* and *rupa* is not a concrete, solid structure. It is all empty space but our senses and mind perceive the forms and give them names. In time, all these change, but the eternal Reality remains unaffected. This, in brief, is the description of Advaita.

Shankaracharya did not lay much emphasis on the "unreality" of the universe, but on the unreality of the individual. All is a continuous flow of consciousness or Reality called Brahman. But we lend it names and forms. This includes the "we." That is, our perception of ourselves as "individuals" is also a phenomenon in maya. We are not individuals. We are that Reality. So Shankaracharya said that this "ego," or "I" of yours, is unreal. Instead of saying that the world you perceive is unreal, Shankara

beyond the beyond. People understand that Brahman is the infinite Reality. But there is a problem. Our minds, unfortunately, are also matter. Mind is matter and thinks in terms of matter. For us, Brahman is vast or infinite, undoubtedly. But this vastness is like the ocean, for instance, or like the sky. We think that physically, Brahman is something big. All our conceptualizations are physical, based on physical limitations we have. This is not altogether bad, however. Advaitic meditation uses the symbols of the ocean or the sky to envision Brahman. But what is important is to know that Brahman is a dot also. That is, the Infinite exists in a physical dot, too. The moment we have to think of Brahman as a tiny dot, we become confused. Can we compare the Infinite with a tiny dot? This is the physical understanding of Brahman.

Limitlessness, expansiveness, or vastness with regards to Brahman, is not physical. This also means that such qualifications are not qualities of Brahman, as they are all just our physical concepts. We say someone is beautiful, handsome, huge, etc. These are qualifications at the material level. But when we speak of Brahman as vast, we are mentioning something strange. We are being informed that Brahman has no qualifications at all. That name, "Brahman", too, is "physical." It has no name or shape or anything. *Guna* means "quality," but not in the earthly sense of qualities. A good bike, for instance, is the quality of the bike. Brahman has no such a quality. When you think of some qualification, guna, you are already limiting That. Anything, for that matter, limits the very idea of the limitless. Yet within the framework of the world in which we live, we have to see that which is beyond through these lenses alone and there is no other way. Therefore, unable to "comprehend" the Reality called Brahman which is beyond thought or mind, we paint It with some qualifications: It Exists, It is Bliss, It is Consciousness.

Of all the schools of Vedanta, Advaita especially, concentrates on Brahman which is beyond gunas or forms. The only thing they say about Brahman is that it is *Sat-chit-ananda*. The other terms, used to give us some idea of that Reality, are all negative. That which is beyond gunas is called *nirguna*. Let's remember one thing: A man without good qualities is a bad man, but Brahman is no deity or God or any such thing. It is beyond this duality of good and bad. Everything which we "think" of is related to the dualistic universe of name and form. The Reality is beyond all this. So it is nirguna and *nirakara* — beyond qualities or qualifications, and formless. These are qualifications for us, so as to have some concrete idea and form for us through which to perceive that Reality. The moment you give forms to Reality, you are considering it to be material. So you miss the point altogether.

Thus Vedanta teaches us about the Reality, which is beyond mind, thought, senses — everything. All we know about It is that it exists. This is the qualification-less Brahman. It is consciousness. We should be cautious here. That Brahman about which Vedanta speaks is nothing material or mental. It is beyond everything. There are some who speak of "formless God." That is completely different. For those who are interested, "God Theory," by Bernard Haisch, will be of immense help in understanding this Vedantic concept of Brahman.

However, Vedanta is not just about Advaita. If everyone has to imagine something which is virtually "unimaginable," it will be difficult to live. You cannot think of air, even though it has some effects which can be imagined. When it comes to this Reality, it is completely nirguna — beyond all qualifications. Even Its "being" ness is not like our earth being there for sometime. It is beyond being and non-being, and so on. If we insist on the formless, quality-less Brahman, we must harshly exclude almost 99% of humanity from knowing the Truth. You may ask, why is it so important to know the Truth? The answer is simple: we are that Truth. Knowledge here is Self-knowledge. We move about without knowing anything about ourselves. We move about like machines. But we aren't machines. And there are no quick ways of knowing the truth about ourselves. Thus Vedanta compassionately speaks of the Reality. But the way Advaita Vedanta wants us to see the manifested universe and the Reality behind as beyond all gunas, makes it hard for countless people.

How can this be resolved? Vedanta does not insist on *Nirguna* Brahman alone. It speaks of other ways of looking at Reality too. The same ocean can be observed from diverse vantage points, and all of them are observing the same ocean.

Vedanta speaks of Brahman with qualifications or qualities, called *Saguna*. This may be confusing. How can that which is beyond become involved? The point is, beyond and within the creation are all our limitations. Further, whatever we may think of, we use our brains and mind only. So Brahman is also saguna, with qualities. What are these qualities? That He, She, or It has forms, names, beauty, glory, goodness, love, etc.

And especially the last one — love. Yes, Love changes everything. A beautiful example of Sri Ramakrishna says it all. There is something called emotion in the human heart. It generates love. This love works wonders. It can solidify water. This water is Brahman. There are regions, says Sri Ramakrishna, where ice does not melt. This unmelting ice is Brahman with name and form, due to the love of the devotee.

Brahman, the Reality, is pure Consciousness. However, when we speak of the saguna aspect of Brahman, we are speaking of the same Brahman with qualifications. Who gave these qualifications? The answer is, who must give them? It is wrong to imagine that Brahman can be this alone and not that. This again is a materialistic limitation, created by our minds. Nobody can limit That about which we know nothing and, amazingly, order Reality to be only this or that.

Thus Brahman can be both qualified and non-qualified. The non-qualified or nirguna is for those who don't wish to think of Reality as "god." The most misused and used word "God," is not God of the judging type. It is the *antaryamin*, the Indweller, who guides the soul and who is the Self of the self. It is love that brings the soul closer to That. So while the advaitic person will not adore with love and affection but shall wish to meditate on infinity, there are others who love to think of the same Brahman as filled with qualities, loving, and so on. The qualified or saguna form of Brahman is for the millions who wish to hold on to something concrete, so that they can pray, worship, adore, and shower their heart's love.

Thus, Saguna and Nirguna, the two paths to the same Reality, are the methods in which we try to understand the incomprehensible. Even as we continue our struggle to comprehend the Divine, we evolve.

Life is a blessed journey from unreality to that Reality. Vedanta teaches us that it is not attained just by one path or one way, but by several, or many. The secret is to create a philosophy for ourselves, have our own ideas of God, the world, and of ourselves, and continue with our spiritual struggle to know the Truth.

Swami Sunirmalananda is a sannyasin of the Ramakrishna Order, and the monk in-charge of the Vedanta Society of Holland. He is Swami Bhuteshanandaji's disciple. The Swami had the privilege of serving his guru for a decade before serving the Ramakrishna Order's centers in Brasil and Geneva.

Empowering Language with Transcendental Wisdom

A Guide for Consciously Creating Experience

The ancient and contemporary teachers of higher Awareness assert that the language we use in daily life is a direct reflection and representation of the paradigm and perspective we hold in our minds about Reality. Our moment-to-moment personal commentary about life's phenomena reveals our idea of who we think we are, what the Universe is, and what the relationship is between these two, if one thinks any exists. One of the essential threads of many spiritual systems of philosophy is that we are eternally empowered to choose how we experience life in relativity or, as we will discuss later, life accompanied by subjective-awareness. Hearing, meditating on, and utilizing a profound vocabulary allows us connect to the Universal Mind *(Mahat)* and live from Freedom rather than a distorted or false idea of self, separation, and resultant extraneous suffering.

English and many other languages, especially in the realm of the physical sciences, have done a remarkable job of describing the physical reality via categories and the transition between them. The seemingly limitless scientific discoveries and advancing technology have been driven in large part by modern language and precise mathematical description of relative processes. While many of us enjoy the comforts and conveniences ultimately derived from modern language, if we are not careful, we can fall into limiting ideas individually and collectively which can lead to fear, confusion, and chaos. In this article, I will explore how to empower daily language with Transcendental Truth. The English words along with discussion are explored in no particular order, and using a somewhat shotgun approach. These serve as examples for any seeker in finding illuminating vocabulary and ways of thinking, regardless of language or culture. Through this practice, the goal is to shift our thinking in how we experience life so as not to limit or immobilize ourselves as we go through the inevitable fluctuations and changes. Becoming skilled at this helps us to realize of the Divine Self we eternally are.

Faith and Belief

When the topic of religion, spirituality, and even science comes up in casual conversation, I have noticed over the years that people tend to use words like faith, belief, or even hope in regard to what they think Truth or God is. Fear of offending, competing, or having to defend one's perspective around Truth might often lead people to using this vocabulary out of social correctness. Such ideas seem indicative of the idea that Truth is either unknowable, requires blind faith to fully comprehend, or that differing views about God must necessarily be in conflict. Many concepts from the Eastern Thinking can help resolve these potential challenges.

Sri Ramakrishna, who was witnessed to have practiced many different religions, described them as various paths up the mountain of Truth. In Eastern Spirituality, a school of Philosophy is called a *darshana*, or way of clear seeing. Some *darshanas* describe Truth as having two modes, depending on one's level of consciousness. An example of this is *Saguna Brahman*, Relative Reality or Reality associating with attributes, and *Nirguna Brahman*, Absolute Reality or Reality without any attributes. These are thought to be two modes of the same Truth. *Saguna Brahman* is as much the Truth as *Nirguna Brahman* just like when an old radio in mono mode is as much a radio when in stereo mode.  If we keep this in mind, we can get at the idea that this Truth can express itself through many approaches, such as Christianity, Islam, or Buddhism as well as the many seers such as Christ, Buddha, or Mohammed. If we know that *Saguna Brahman* is a limitless expression of the Truth, but that in doing this expression, It never changes, we arrive at a place of acceptance and understanding which roots out our individual tendency to want to be right, superior, or compare. It doesn't ultimately matter in what way God/Truth appears or appeals to various beings. Affirming that the Truth exists, It can be known, and beings go along their path towards It, is likely a more settling, harmonizing, and universal way to look at the spiritual journey of humanity and the Reality. So, we can try substituting ways of clear seeing over faith or belief, as often used in the realm of these various Eastern philosophies.

Objectivity

The notion of being objective or free of subjective/individual bias in interpreting events is another prominent notion in Western Science, Philosophy, and other disciplines. The idea of being objective seems to suggest there is way to reason and experience that is free from the overlay of one's individuality. Related to this, Eastern Psychology explains that the mind, which is the foundation of the Universe and how we experience it, is by nature endowed with the ego-mechanism, ahamkara. This is sometimes translated as separate-I-maker. This part of the mind is responsible for the idea of being a separate individual existing in time and space. Only those beings who have had experiences of super-consciousness, samadhi, which are devoid of ahamkara, can say they have gone beyond subjective experience and bias, and thus experienced Truth in a direct sense. This is known as the eternal Subject. It is experienced when the division between subject and object vanishes.

While this might sound demotivating, it's actually extremely empowering. When we know our sense of individual or subject is conditioning our experience, but that this essential ingredient can be consciously chosen, we become increasingly masters over our life since we realize we are projecting it via this choice. Many systems of the wisdom traditions such as Vedanta, Yoga, Tantra, and Buddhism provide methods for this. For example, in Vedanta, one meditates on the five sheaths of the Atman: physical body, vital energy, mind, intellect, and bliss. A person who has not practiced this might experience life as being the body and mind only, most likely thinking these are separate and also identifying with them. Their idea of themselves is probably distorted and compartmentalized, rather than integrated where one has a full view of the mechanism of experience, i.e. the five sheaths, and knowing their true essence, the Self, to be separate from, yet permeating them. Hence their choice of subject is necessarily limiting. But, through such systems, we can make less limiting choices, where we have integrated and understood these five, but know the Self to be none of them. Thus, it might be more informative to say consciously-chosen-subjectivity. Our individual lens for personal experience can be chosen so that it forms the doorway to ultimate freedom and Self-Realization. Beyond objectivity lies the eternal Subject and Truth.

seeds to all knowledge. Our individual mind (*antahkarana*) is thought to be connected to the *Mahat* similar to how a sub radio station is connected to the actual radio station. Lastly, Swami Vivekananda stated that concentration is a necessary condition for learning, and that concentration comes from us. The point of this is that we might find it strengthening to consider accounting for ourselves as the most important ingredient in activating or manifesting knowledge in our minds. A practitioner might try out the words uncovering, revealing, or allowing, as a substitute for learning and growth. The fact being that we already have all knowledge in potential, and that what we call learning is really to bring forth the knowledge into form. This way we do not fall into illogical ideas of acquiring, building, or creating something out of nothing. A personal favorite in my journey has been to think of manifesting inherent knowledge. "Inherent" is such a powerful English word, since it pertains to characteristics or aspects of something that are the very inseparable nature of it. For example, we can say that heaviness in inherent in lead. Some *slokas* from the *Bhagavad Gita* point to the notion of knowledge being inherent within the Self, such as:

(3:38-9) *As fire is enveloped by smoke, as a mirror by dust, as an embryo by the womb, so is this inherent knowledge covered by desire.*

(5:16) *Shining like the sun, knowledge reveals the Supreme in them, whose ignorance is destroyed by Self-knowledge.*

> "We fall into ideas that we are our bodies, minds, accomplishments, resumes, God's judgement, and other potentially weakening notions. As we learn, we think that our knowledge is acquired from a place outside of ourselves, like acquiring gold from a mine. Many also think of knowledge as being created from a previous state of non-existence — like how we conventionally think of an inventor inventing an invention, thinking that it had no prior existence."

Learning and Growth

Conventional upbringing and life inundates and inculcates in us with the idea of change, along with the necessity of growth and learning. We think of ourselves as ever developing, as our bodies and minds go through various stages, and that striving to improve is a must in order to survive and prosper. We fall into ideas that we are our bodies, minds, accomplishments, resumes, God's judgement, and other potentially weakening notions. As we learn, we think that our knowledge is acquired from a place outside of ourselves, like acquiring gold from a mine. Many also think of knowledge as being created from a previous state of non-existence — like how we conventionally think of an inventor inventing an invention, thinking that it had no prior existence, even as an idea within the Universal Mind (*Mahat*).

In contrast, *"you cannot get something from nothing"* has been the stance of Eastern Thinking for millennia. Additionally, in Patanjali's *Yoga*, the Universal Mind (*Mahat*), is said to contain the

Sin, Guilt, and Shame

The notion of sin is perhaps one of the most emotionally charged concepts derived from religion. For many, it drums up experiences of guilt, shame, fire-and-brimstone fundamentalist preaching, and the prime necessity to fix or cleanse oneself due to being born sinful by nature, and therefore deficient and defective. These ideas are not just limited to the realm of religion, but also can be seen in modern secular religionists with their notions of authoritarian political correctness. Here, the idea of sin gets applied in the workplace, online, public life, academic institutions, and virtually all areas of societal life via approved behaviors and words. Using the wrong words, body language, or gestures could get one fired or cancelled, as we see happening in current pop culture and media. The idea is the same, in that if you do the "wrong" things you are a sinner and deserve to be punished and ostracized.

How could something perfect become imperfect? If the soul

> "If the soul were to become imperfect due to sin, from a previous state of perfection, such assertion seems to contradict the idea that the soul was perfect in the first place. How could something perfect, commit a sin or do something 'wrong?' Even if we vibrate at the realm of thinking where we attribute the creation act to a perfect, all-powerful, all-pervasive, all-knowing God, how could It create anything that is imperfect?"

were to become imperfect due to sin, from a previous state of perfection, such assertion seems to contradict the idea that the soul was perfect in the first place. How could something perfect, commit a sin or do something "wrong?" Even if we vibrate at the realm of thinking where we attribute the creation act to a perfect, all-powerful, all-pervasive, all-knowing God, how could It create anything that is imperfect? These types of questions, which many of us asked as children, suggest that the idea of sin might not be the most productive or logical way of looking at our actions and selves.

The question then comes: what is an empowering way to look at actions and results, rather than as sinful or virtuous, right or wrong? In my own journey, it starts with withdrawing from egotistical judgments, coverings, and distortions surrounding the whole matter. This has meant refraining from labeling happenings as good or bad, pleasing or painful. In Indian Philosophy, good and bad are called dualities (*dvandva*). Or more completely stated, dualities like pleasure and pain are interconnected pairs of opposites that are really one and same. Sometimes this gets punctuated as good-bad, or pleasure-pain, for emphasis. Ruminating on *dvandva*, can give rise to *dvandvamohena*, delusion from the pairs of opposites. This can cause us to fall into fallacious ideas about ourselves and the nature of the Soul. So, as we perform actions in daily life, results are being sown, because that is the way Relativity works. Cause-and-effect is a fact of the Universe. When contemplating our works, we can look at the result as potentially useful, but noisy (not 100% accurate) data, that may point us towards correcting our course along the path of increased wisdom, love, fulfillment, and Self-realization. If we subject our actions and thoughts to the lens of Self-knowledge by cognizing the Soul as perfect and ultimately not in the field of activity, all actions become a revelation of the Self. We begin to infer the Self, as the Witness and Substratum, for all works and thoughts (*pratibodhaviditam*), as discussed in the *Kena Upanisad*. This new viewpoint represents a healthy practice of non-attachment. We have a benign curiosity and interest in our actions, like a scientist running an experiment, who trusts that eventually his work will reveal Nature's secrets.

Categories of Separation

As previously discussed in the second paragraph of this article, modern language, particularly that of science, tends to cut our experience up into categories via the classification process. This can have a conditioning effect on our minds, where we believe all of relative experience to function through separateness. We think we are separate from others and various objects, and are unaware of an interconnectedness of life (*yoga*). Quantum Physics has disproved the idea of separation in a physical sense, but thinking of experience in terms of divine principles or *tattvas*, may provide a more integrated perspective. The term divine principle has many profound implications, but the overall idea is that the Universe is made up of and experienced through a series of interconnected evolutes out of the Cosmic Mind. These evolutes ultimately involute back to their source. Nothing in the relative realm is experienced in isolation when these divine principles are acknowledged and understood. Readers might study the 24 Cosmic Principles of the *Samkhya* Philosophy for further details. While it may seem obvious, hatred, fear, and craving naturally diminish when we see life via connected divine principles rather than through categories and labels of separation.

Conclusion

I have attempted in this article to share some empowering vocabulary and teachings in the context of common ideas present within the mind of collective humanity. Exploring these conventional viewpoints and the philosophical implications of such notions can lead to some profound, if not sobering conclusions. With the core teachings from Eastern Philosophy, such as Vedanta, one can find a more flexible way to interpret and construct meaning from experiences while associating with the Subjective/Relative Plane. Readers are encouraged to bolster their Truth-vocabulary, that is, find concepts that leave Reality and the Self in a place of eternal unchanging perfection and limitless abundance and expression. This will lead to increased awareness, self-revelation, self-integration, peace, and harmony for oneself and the benefit of others.

Brother Tadrupa Josh McDaniel is an initiated student of SRV Associations. He has studied with Babaji Bob Kindler for eight years. Tadrupa serves as an advisor to the SRV Board of Directors and assists with various activities such as classes, retreats, and secretarial duties. In his professional life, Tadrupa enjoys serving and coaching students as a college math instructor.

SHEIKH NUR AL JERRAHI

UNDERSTANDING ISLAM

When asked once why he had undertaken to become a Sheikh of the Jerrahi Order, accepting the great responsibility for its line of dervishes, and thereby embracing a Muslim path, Lex Hixon answered simply and in part that as there were so many millions of Muslims in the world, there was therefore a great need for undertstanding them and their religion. A bridge was needed, he averred, that would close the gap between the world and this youngest of the world's great religions and bring its tenets into full view for the good of all humanity. This article is excerpted from an interview given while Lex was still living.

The Sheikh of a Sufi Order has the "permission" and the ability to interpret dreams. What does that entail? Let's go right to the heart of the matter. Our conventional mind is reflected outside as the conventional society. The spiritual path is the pathway where we gradually emancipate ourself from the limited self and the limited society, which are co-relatives. In a compassionate way, though, we're not leaving humanity behind. We want to manifest in a way which is even more compassionate and skillful, precisely in order to be of service to humanity. The question then becomes how to step around our limited self, how to "tame" it or "fool" it to the point where one can become emancipated from it. Dreams are a very, very helpful way to do this, because in dream the psyche is not working on an ordinary conscious level and great wisdom can be manifested in these dreams.

Analysis and Intuition

In the Sufi orders, we are not like psychoanalysts at all. We have a totally different approach, feeling that some dreams come from Allah, from God, from the Source of Truth, and other dreams are just a function of the psyche. We make a distinction between those two categories, and we deal primarily with revelatory dreams. The way we interpret them is not by a set of dream symbols, so that one thing always equals another, but it's what you might call a charismatic form of interpretation. When someone tells me a dream, whatever comes into my mind I give as the interpretation. I'll give you an example of that.

My sheikh from Istanbul, Muzaffer, once was with his sheikh, who was a great adept at dream interpretation. Two people came with the same dream. Each person dreamt that they climbed the minaret and gave the Islamic call to prayer. To the first person, the sheikh said, "Congratulations, you're going to go on a pilgrimage this year to Mecca and Medina. Prepare yourself." To the second person he said, "You've taken something that doesn't belong to you. Find out what it is and give it back." That completely leaves behind anything that's a rational or single-oriented dream interpretation. Not everyone is permitted to do that. That's very, very important, because dream interpretation is not considered something that you can just study and then sort of set up shop and become an expert. In my case, the way the effendi taught me the dream interpretation was not through a seminar, and not through discussions. He put his turban on my head and prayed to Allah that I be able to interpret dreams; then he took the turban off. It was very swift. I thought he might leave the turban on a while and let it soak in, but....

The Power of Direct Experience

When I performed the "Hajj," the pilgrimage to Mecca that I wrote about in *The Heart of the Koran*, a couple of important dreams took place there. Probably the most interesting was that before I even reached the sacred city of Mecca, where the Kabba is situated, we were in Medina, which is the other sacred city in Saudi Arabia where the prophet Mohammed — upon him be peace — ended his days, and his sacred remains are there. Before even reaching the goal of pilgrimage I had a dream. I gave the dream to the effendi and he interpreted: "Your pilgrimage has been accepted." So even before I made it, it was accepted. Many of the people who were there, when they heard this interpretation, wept because of the energy of the interpretation; it was so strong. It was not just somebody saying, "I think this is what it means." The energy of the interpretation itself is part of the revelatory dream. A dream is like a lock, and the interpretation is like the key. When they meet together, correctly, something opens and there's a flash of recognition on the part of the dreamer and everyone else who happens to be present.

The Friends of Allah

The founder of our order is Sultan Mohammed Nureddin Jerrahi, who disappeared from physical eyes in 1721. He is one of our great saints, one of what we call the "Friends of Allah." They awaken as the divine qualities, they awaken as the divine life itself, as the divine beauty; so when they die physically, where do they go? They're still here in the form of this unique configuration of the divine attributes. Every soul is a unique configuration of the divine attributes. Therefore, the souls are not interchangeable in that sense, but also there is no entity in that sense called a "soul." Ultimately, it is just God, the attributes of God weaving a tapestry, you might say, a unique tapestry. So Nureddin Jerrahi, may his secret be guarded — this is the way we refer to a great saint, because we feel that the saints have such profound spiritual secrets that the religion and society in general are not ready to uncover them. So, Nureddin Jerrahi, may his secret be guarded, is absolutely with us and with our order now, and in fact he's standing in the center of all the mystic Dervish circles of all the orders in the world of Islam today, as are all the great saints.

For me personally, my two great guides were Sheikh Muzaffer of Istanbul, and Bawa Muhaiyaddeen, a sheikh from Sri Lanka, whom I met in 1973 when he came to Philadelphia. He was and is very, very unique. He passed away from visible eyes, from our ordinary visible vision, in 1986, shortly after Muzaffer effendi passed away. His holy tomb is outside Philadelphia in the countryside. It's the first major tomb of a Sufi saint to be here in the U.S., with the exception of Sufi Sam Lewis, whose holy tomb is at the Lama Foundation in New Mexico. So we have one native-born Sufi master whose holy tomb is here and one great Sufi master from the East whose holy tomb is here. The tombs of Islamic saints are very, very significant because they're like crystal sets. Their physical remains remain uncorrupt, that is, not decaying in an ordinary sense. They operate as crystal transmissions. Of course, their souls have melted into the divine attributes. So they're not there in their tombs in the ordinary sense, but these crystal sets are there, and they're very important places for making spiritual progress.

Understanding Sufism and Islam

People often get confused about Sufism and Islam, and ask what is the difference. What if you asked Saint Francis, "What is the connection between what you're doing and Christianity?" He would be puzzled. He wouldn't even really know what you were asking. The Sufi orders in Islam were founded by people like Saint Francis and became like the Franciscan order. They were founded by people who were so deeply immersed in Islam that they didn't see anything in the universe but a kind of universal Islam. They saw the Christians and Jews and all of the other devout peoples as being truly submitted, ones who are surrendering themselves to the Source of life with every breath, with every movement. For them, it was a kind of universal Islam. So, in that sense, the Sufis shouldn't be identified with any sort of narrow-minded Islam, or with any cultural chauvinistic Islam, but definitely with Islam itself. Sufism and Islam are one.

The very definition for the word Islam is revealing. There are so many imaginative etymologies that people use. I came up with one spontaneously myself, a modern etymology. By the permutation of letters, which is natural in Arabic and with the Kabbalists of Judaism to understand the meaning of words, I say that Sufism means "Fusion."

The Spiritual Constellations

As to the various saints of Islam, and the Sufi saints as well, the idea is that the whole sky of Sufism is full of countless constellations and galaxies and planets and heavenly bodies, all in one sky. That sky is the supreme Consciousness, the only consciousness that we call Allah, the Truth. In that sense, it's difficult to conceive any of them as being outside the sky. Each one is one of the heavenly bodies, as it were, part of the heavenly body of the spheres.

Yet, if you talked to various Sufis or Muslims you might get down to a level where they have certain gripes with each other, certain differences of opinion, which is only natural. That's part of the limited society. I call it the "limited religion," which is just another correlation of the limited self. I don't have any arguments with anyone who is promoting the elevation of all mankind and who regards humanity, as the holy Koran reveals, as *"the crown of creation."* Our humanity is not something insignificant in creation. It's the crown. My mother is a religious skeptic. I've been debating with her ever since I was a young boy. She used to say: "Humanity is just like this little ant on a little tiny rock in the middle of nowhere. How can they assume that they know God, and all of this, and even know what God's will is?" "But, Mom," I would counter, "what kind of ant can figure out that there are a hundred million galaxies out there? That's a very unusual ant. If you find an ant that knows that there are a hundred million galaxies, please tell me."

And what kind of ant receives holy testament through the revealed scriptures? The Holy Koran is the sole scripture of Islam, with 6,666 verses. There are great mysteries about it. For instance, the physical, historical Koran, which is this book with these many verses, is considered a mirror reflection of the universal Koran, which is the universe itself. The universal Koran is considered a mirror reflection of the infinite awareness of Allah. We cannot possibly become fundamentalists about this book if we have the illumination of the Sufi tradition.

Short of the fundamentalism of the religionists, there is also this intolerance and narrowness among the worldly peoples. Islam today, to bring it more into a political and social context, is not getting a very good press. Westerners are not sensitively educated or even accurately informed about Islam. I think it's part of the global civilization that is emerging; it's one of the gaps. How long was it that the United Nations didn't accept mainland China? One billion human beings! It was a kind of cultural gap that was caused by certain historical problems, like the United States not wanting to give recognition where it was due. So, refusing to recognize the one billion Muslims in the world is a kind of myopia of Western civilization which rather soon, inshallah [God willing], will disappear, just like China's powerful presence was finally admitted into the U.N.

World-view and World-civilization

Transcendent of fundamentalism and secularism, there is the Islamic or Sufi world-view. Islam is a coherent world civilization wherein a cohesion exists between a peasant farming rice in Bangladesh, a shepherd herding sheep in the Rif mountains of Morocco, and an American-born Muslim in New York City. There are not only thousands of miles in distance between these three, but there are also tremendous cultural disparities — yet they all share in the faith equally. They're all on the same wavelength. The Koran is precisely that wavelength. To have something which is the sole scripture, the sole representative of all the levels of Islam, from the most sophisticated to the most direct and simple, is a very positive thing. It does not mean that all these levels are easily recognizable in the Koran. It's a lifetime study. But I would say definitely that this aforementioned shepherd and farmer, and also some 200 people, most of them North Americans that belong to our mosque in New York city, for instance, are all on the same wavelength. It's what I call an ancient mind, and the ancient mind is extremely flexible so that the ancient mind can get along perfectly well with modern technology and civilization. The Tibetan lamas love to carry around electronics, and the Dalai Lama takes apart radios and watches and things like that just for a hobby. There's no contradiction between the ancient mind and modern civilization.

For instance, take for example the phrase, "*La illah ilallah Mohammed rasullah*" which is frequently chanted in Sufi ceremonies. What does it mean? It's the affirmation of the divine unity, in Arabic. We feel it is really at the heart of every conscious being, at the center of every atom in creation, and that this unity alone exists. This is the radical view of the Sufis, the traditional affirmation of Islam, "la illah etc." which means "the one God alone is worthy of worship, and Mohammed is his messenger." That's re-envisioned in Sufism or re-experienced to mean that only God exists, that only the One exists, and that Mohammed, that is, humanity, is Its conscious self-expression.

Dervish Practices

In "zikr," one of our sacred rituals, the dervishes make the circle and they begin repeating, "La illah ilallah," and at that point there's a high degree of receptivity and that divine oneness begins to blossom consciously in the hearts and minds of the dervishes at that time. It causes ecstasy in some, brilliant clarity and wisdom and awareness in others, all depending on the temperament of each dervish. "Zikr," is remembrance, but it's more; you might forget your telephone number, even though you know it very well. You remember it, but you might forget it. But you don't ever forget that you exist. That kind of absolute deep remembrance, when we apply it to God, we become God, not forgetting Himself. That's what we mean by remembrance.

At an SRV Retreat in Woodstock, N.Y., taught by spiritual director, Babaji Bob Kindler, Sheikh Nur Al Jerrahi (Lex Hixon) leads the group of retreat participants in an oudoor, free-style Zikir on the ample grounds of the 100 acre SRV National Temple and Retreat Center.

Reciting "La illah ilallah" 700 times a day constitutes divine remembrance as well. 700 is symbolic of the seven levels of awareness that constitute the Sufi path leading from less refined to more refined until finally, on the seventh level, there is only the divine awareness. Among other practices, awareness of breathing, also present in other religions and their practices, is there in Sufism as well. But people might think that we have "breath exercises," but that's really in the area of inducing experiences, so we don't look upon the breath as some sort of great special mystique. The point is that the divine breath is life itself. In our zikr we often repeat the divine name "Ya Hai," meaning the All-Living One, so we might be chanting, "hai, hai, hai," like that, and it might look to people from the outside as if that's some sort of breathing exercise. We don't think of it as breath, we think of it as divine life.

Then there's the prayers. Five times a day prayers are the blessed core of Islam that also flowers in the Sufi way. But the Sufis again have a slightly different view of it. We feel that we aren't doing the prayers, but that Allah is doing the prayers. It all proceeds from the heart. In the science of Sufism there are nine hearts, each within each other. The physical heart is like the Kabba. For instance, in Mecca there is this stone cube where we orient our prayers on the pilgrimage, but no one is praying to the stone. Similarly we orient our zikr towards our physical heart, in that direction, and as we look in that direction spiritually, with the eyes of the heart, we see nine hearts extending, that is, if we had the opportunity to see the whole picture, each heart is more refined and subtle, and finally the secret heart is the heart of God.

The Science of Sufism

Sufism is a great science. For fourteen centuries now the Islamic mystics have been very active, somehow more active than possibly Christian and maybe even Jewish mystics. There's been actually greater freedom for Islamic mystics to function in, even though there have been times of persecution. So, we have fourteen centuries, and none of these books have been burned — or if they have been in certain places, they still exist in other places. We haven't lost anything in fourteen centuries of research of the most highly disciplined, highly gifted spiritual beings of not just one culture, but all the cultures on the planet. As a result we have a huge body of scientific research available. And unlike some theological beliefs, Islam does not teach that the soul is somehow miraculously created at the time of conception, or shortly thereafter. Rather, Islam feels that the soul is created in pre-eternity. Therefore it has already heard the Koran, it has already received all of that wisdom, and it's just unfolded naturally along the path of Islam.

Lex Hixon (Nur al-Jerrahi) received his Ph.D. in World Religions from Columbia University in 1976. He then became an adept practitioner of several of the world's sacred traditions. From 1971 to 1984 he conducted a weekly radio show in New York City called "In The Spirit," interviewing spiritual teachers from around the world. An enlightened spiritual teacher, he guided many souls along their chosen path. Among his books are *Great Swan, Mother of the Universe, Heart of the Koran, Atom from the Sun of Knowledge, Mother of the Buddhas,* and *Living Buddha Zen.* For more information inquire at: www.lexhixon.org

They Who Know Us

With hidden Wisdom in the being of Truth
you know us.

In the endless ocean of secret knowledge
you know us.

The nightingales of this temporal garden
will not hear us.

Lovers of the beauty of His Eternal Face
will know us.

We care not to rebuild this world
or the next.

Those who stumble and are ruined
will know us.

We left our senses, dropped the cloak
from our shoulders

Strip yourself bare, be naked
to know us.

They suffer who do not know that pain and joy
are one.

The sultan saved from torment
knows us.

The hermit who stays sober
will not understand us.

One drunk on the last gulp of the wine of purity
will know us.

It is for man to heed the wise one's
every word.

Do not suppose that those who live like animals
will know us.

We are but a drop that fell in the ocean
today.

What knowledge can a drop
possess?

Only the ocean
knows us.

*Poem selected from "The Unveiling of Love,"
by Sheikh Muzaffer Ozak Al-Jerrahi*

DISCRIMINATION BETWEEN THE ABSOLUTE & THE RELATIVE

Clarification of Vedantic Terms and Truisms

In the scripture, *Vivekachudamani*, The *Crest Jewel of Discrimination*, the great *Advaitin*, Shankaracharya, states, "*It is the apt and final conclusion of the Vedanta that all is Brahman – time, space, living beings, and the world. Living in constant realization of this is what is called Enlightenment. Brahman is one without a second, pure and perfect, and the revealed scriptures are the sure and certain proof of this fact.*" Hearing this nondual truth at the beginning of the spiritual path is a great boon, for then we know our intended spiritual destination.

Depending on where, how, and by whom the first teaching is given, however, the supporting teachings that make the path comprehensive may be left out of the picture. It is important to know that there is more to learn! There is much, especially for Westerners, that has to be learned, as well as unlearned, before the truth of *Advaita* is fully understood, even intellectually. Further, reliance on intellectual understanding alone, without the requisite moral and ethical virtues, will be fruitless. Greed, anger, selfishness, jealousy, lust, pride, arrogance, laziness, impatience, weakness, insecurities, fear, etc., all these will distort the intellect in gross and subtle ways, preventing a true comprehension of the Vedantic teachings.

When people hear about nonduality for the first time and intuit the glory and preeminence of this rare perspective, they often undergo a reevaluation of the world around them, their personal life, and relationships, their actions and tendencies, their sufferings and those of others. Receiving the knowledge of the illumined beings that all existence is one, homogenous, blissful Reality, and everything we experience with senses and mind, is unreal like a dream, questions and confusions might arise. How does the one become the many? Why did I leave blissful oneness for dreams of pain and suffering?

Those who are enjoying their lives may rejoice in the idea of Oneness with all, and mistaking it for that buoyant sensation arising in the heart, then cast that pleasurable feeling over phenomena with subtle or not so subtle attachment upon the world. "Life is good; I am one with everything." On the other hand, those who are caught in a cycle of suffering wonder who to blame for it, since the world and karma are a dream – "Who's dream?" We need to understand the *dharma* teachings in order to hold both the Absolute (nonduality) and the relative (the physical and mental realms and our experiences in them) in their proper perspectives.

Taking the teachings of Vedanta via the traditional method from a qualified teacher and studying the Vedantic scriptures ensures that one has the tools and guidance to practice the foundational and essential method of Vedanta: Discrimination between the Self and the non-Self. "Following the tradition" means to develop one's character, humbly take the teachings from a qualified teacher, and follow his or her instructions regarding spiritual disciplines and their application in life to the best of one's ability. Further, we are encouraged to have the strength and verve of those rare individuals who radically turn their entire mind to God and/or, the patience of the ancient practitioner who vowed to empty the ocean drop by drop with a feather.

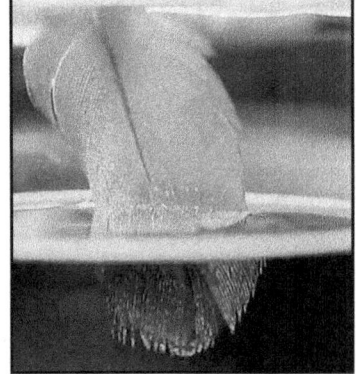

"*Now, when we study metaphysics, we come to know the world is one, not that the spiritual, the material, the mental, and the world of energies are separate. It is all one, but seen from different planes of vision. When you think of yourself as a body, you forget that you are a mind, and when you think of yourself as a mind, you will forget the body. There is only one thing, that you are; you can see it either as matter or body – or you can see it as mind or spirit. Birth, life, and death are but old superstitions. None was ever born; none will ever die; one changes one's position – that is all.*" - Swami Vivekananda, "Hints on Practical Spirituality," Home of Truth

Recognizing one's position, as Swami Vivekananda mentions above, is something practitioners learn as they study the philosophy and revealed scriptures. In Vedanta, we are told the truth of Nonduality at the start, and then follow it up with knowledge of what the non-Self is. This knowledge allows us to recognize the non-Self and make corrections to our thinking. The dharma teachings are part of the cosmology and philosophy, which are like the rungs of a ladder taking us from conventional ways of thinking and behavior that create karma and suffering in relative life, to illumined mind that has a clear understanding of the Absolute and its immutability. Before we are grounded in these "rungs," we will make erroneous conclusions or experience doubts under at least three headings: Mixing up the Absolute and Relative perspectives, quandaries arising from missing pieces of cosmology, and confusion due to the failure to recognize different philosophical perspectives.

Before addressing some of the questions that often arise, let us see how Swami Vivekananda introduced the philosophical basis of the Oneness of Advaita (the Absolute) in his lecture on "The Absolute & Manifestation," from the *Jnana Yoga* lectures:

> "The Advaita Vedanta of Indian philosophy is a sea change of perspective when grasped properly, not to mention realized in actuality. The illumined beings who attain this rare atmosphere are no longer confused by anything in relativity."

"The one question that is most difficult to grasp in understanding the Advaita philosophy, and the one question that will be asked again and again and that will always remain is: How has the Infinite, the Absolute, become the finite? I will now take up this question, and, in order to illustrate it, I will use a figure. Here is the Absolute (a), and this is the universe (b). The Absolute has become the universe. By this is not only meant the material world, but the mental world, the spiritual world – heavens and earths, and in fact, everything that exists. Mind is the name of a change, and body the name of another change, and so on, and all these changes compose our universe. This Absolute (a) has become the universe (b) by coming through time, space, and causation (c). This is the central idea of Advaita. Time, space, and causation are like the glass through which the Absolute is seen, and when It is seen on the lower side, It appears as the universe. Now we at once gather from this that in the Absolute there is neither time, space, nor causation." – Chapter 6: The Absolute & Manifestation, part of Jnana Yoga lectures.

In common speech, we are constantly confusing the Absolute with the Relative. "I" means one's Self, which we now know is eternal, all-pervasive Spirit/Consciousness. Yet, we commonly say such things as: "I am hungry," "I am overweight," "I am a parent or someone's child," "I am going to some place," "I am happy/angry," "I am suffering and going to die," and so forth. In truth, we are saying we are a body that lives and dies; we are a role that belongs to the body and the mind attached to it, and other related limitations. In every case such language betrays how we unconsciously superimpose the relative over the Absolute, what Vedanta calls *"taking the unreal for the Real."*

The *Advaita Vedanta* of Indian philosophy is a sea of change of perspective when grasped properly, not to mention realized in actuality. The illumined beings who attain this rare atmosphere are no longer confused by anything in relativity. Neither are they at odds with other paths or teachings that lead from lower truth to higher Truth. In fact, they make use of those relative teachings to help others. They do not become "born again nondualists" who reject other pathways that people follow according to their temperament. Sri Ramakrishna would tell his students and visitors to hold fast to God with form if that was their ideal, or God without form if that was their ideal. At the same time, he would also tell them never to cherish the idea that only their view was correct. He would follow this up by saying, *"God is with form, and God is without form, and He is beyond both form and formlessness entirely."* His final statement is the advaitic stance of one with direct experience.

His disciple, Swami Vivekananda, later expressed this same idea as the three stages of philosophy: Dualism, where the seeker feels that God is a separate divine entity; Qualified Nondualism, where the aspirant feels God's presence within and experiences that he is a part of God, the Whole; and finally, Nondualism, where one intuits and finally realizes that there is no separation between the Self and God, and that what has all along been seen as a world has only been that one Reality. These are also the "positions" intimated in Vivekananda's quote above. Over the course of lifetimes we travel along these stages, and the *Upanisads*, *Gita*, other scriptures, and the great Teachers, will speak from these different positions in order to explain the nature of the Soul/Self, the embodied soul, and the world to beings who are at different perspectives, thereby guiding them to deeper realizations. Thus, becoming familiar with each of these positions via scriptures, instruction from a teacher, and contemplation avoids the problem of concluding that the teachings are contradictory.

Let us now take up a few questions that can arise before a comprehensive understanding of Non-duality/Advaita is gained. The purpose for addressing these is less about answering them fully and more about encouraging spiritual practitioners to "follow the Tradition," and study the *dharma* teachings with a teacher.

Why would I leave the Freedom and Bliss of being Brahman (Absolute Reality) to take a body?

The body, senses, mind, intellect, and ego are all part of (b), the universe, in Vivekananda's diagram. When we ask this question, we have taken the position of identifying with the body-mind complex and all its limitations in (b) the universe. We have superimposed the qualities of the relative on "I," which is ultimately found in Brahman/the Absolute. In the Absolute, there is no time, space, and causation. Like all questions posed from the standpoint of relativity concerning the Absolute, there is no ultimate answer. We must shift our perspective to that of Brahman, even intellectually, in order to see there is no actual coming or going. We have always been the Absolute, we only shifted our perspective to the psycho-physical realm and forgotten our true nature – like one sitting in a fog bank in a valley surrounded by mountains glistening in the sun. Spiritual instruction followed by practice are the path leading out of the fogbank.

(a) The Absolute
(c) Time Space Causation
(b) The Universe

If I am ever free and never bound, why am I suffering?

This question arises from the same error of perspective, while also showing that we must understand the relative laws of karma and reincarnation. Some nontraditional teachers of Nondualism want their students to grasp that karma, action, and its results (good or bad), do not exist in the Absolute and are therefore unreal. Knowing this intellectually, however, without learning how the mind creates action and results for itself via desire-based thinking and actions, stymies many such aspirants. This is part of *Yoga Psychology* and a great aid for recognizing habits of thought that lead away from purification of mind so necessary for realization of the Self.

If everything is a dream, then why do my actions matter?

This is a reasonable question if sincere, but worrisome if asked in order to avoid responsibility for selfish, desire-driven actions. In fact, those who know the world is a dream, that is, truly see it as such and the *Atman/Brahman* shining undivided through it all, are imbued with all virtues and do nothing for the sake of the limited self. Desire for enjoyment of earthly objects is transcended in favor of God Consciousness. While one is identified with the body-mind complex, one's actions matter because the sense of ownership, agency, and the sense of being an individual permeates actions with subtle or not so subtle desire for the results. This creates good, bad, and mixed *karma*. Our reactions to these karmic repercussions create more *karmas*. Due to this, one's life and mind are kept in a restless state which is a great obstacle to spiritual attainment. A question like this also arises from not having learned the supporting teachings.

Since I am Brahman, I don't need to do spiritual practices.

Teachers of Vedanta will tell their students, "You are not *Brahman/Atman* until you realize you are Brahman." Though it is true that spiritual practice cannot "make one into Brahman" since Brahman is our Essence already, spiritual practice purifies the mind until it dissolves and *Atman/Brahman* is revealed. The point is that this question arises when we do not know about the mind and its four-fold functions: basic mind (*manas*), intellect (*buddhi*), thoughts (*chitta*), and the ego (*ahamkara*). The result of this ignorance about the mind is that we do not make a distinction between the Self and the mind. Otherwise, we would understand that it is the mind that veils *Brahman*.

If Brahman is all, then nature is real, divine, and Sentient.

For most students, this is a premature conclusion. Although *"Brahman is all – the world, time, and living beings,"* it first needs to be understood the way Swami Vivekananda explained it above. Next, we need to be cautious about superimposing the inherent attributes of the Absolute/Brahman on forms due to attachment. Existence, Knowledge, and Bliss are the very nature of *Brahman*, and without It, nothing would be perceptible to us. It is the *"one Light shining, by which all else shines."* When we see a beautiful landscape or a person we love, can we mentally dissolve the name and form and still "see" Brahman? Or does Brahman disappear to us when the landscape is ravaged by fire or the body of our loved one dies? *Atman-Brahman* is the only Sentient principle; everything else borrows it, just as the moon shines by the borrowed light of the sun. Light does not belong to the moon. Similarly, reality, divinity, and Sentiency belong to *Brahman* and never to the form. Understanding this, then consider Swami Vivekananda's statement: *"God is not in the world, the world is in God."*

How can my mind possibly create the universe?

From Sage Vasishtha, to Lord Buddha, to Sri Sarada Devi, the teaching that the universe is mind made manifest has been stated and explained over the course of at least 5,000 years. To understand this requires the cosmological and philosophical knowledge that there is not just a physical world, but also mental or heavenly worlds, and also the causal state from which these all arise. Each realm is inhabited by beings with minds, and the minds of all beings are part of the Cosmic Mind. Thus, yes, the individual mind does not create the universe by itself, but via collective and Cosmic mind of which it is a part. It is also important to know that the individual mind creates its own individual karmas and mental tendencies, which has a tremendous impact on one's experience of the world

Sometimes "they" say God is everything and then they say God is not a thing.

When "they" refers to the revealed scriptures and the statement of the rishis/seers, and contemporary teachers, it is said from the *Advaitic* perspective: *"Sarvam khalvidam Brahman,"* all this indeed is *Brahman*. When a scripture or seer tells us that God is not a thing, this is stated from either a dualistic or Qualified nondual position to emphasize the fact that God is never limited by a form or concept, being all-pervasive and transcendent of time, space, and causation. All forms come and go, but God/*Brahman* is immutable.

If Brahman/the Absolute is the ultimate Truth, then the Personal God is a myth and I should worship Brahman.

Brahman/Absolute can never be objectified; It is the eternal Seer. Thus, It is not an object of worship. Once the Absolute is viewed through the "glass of time, space, and causation," we find both the *jiva*/individual being and *Ishvara*/Personal God, who is the sum total of all souls and the repository of all beneficent qualities and powers. In the Vedanta philosophy, *Ishvara* is described as controlling *maya*, whereas the *jiva* is under the control of *maya*. The Personal God is co-existent with the individual. As long as one experiences oneself as an individual, *Ishvara* will also exist. The Personal God, *Ishvara* or *Saguna Brahman* (*Brahman* with attributes), is the greatest aid on the way to nondual realization. As Swami Vivekananda has variously explained, *Ishvara* is the highest concept of God possible to the human mind. Though not often stated, *Ishvara* is both with form and without form. Further, as long as one remains at the intellectual frame of reference, even the concept of nondual Reality is a manifestation of that *Ishvara*. When the individual self merges in the nondual *Brahman*, *Ishvara* also dissolves there.

God is actionless vs. God is the only doer.

The Absolute is immutable, timeless, spaceless. Again, drawing on Swami Vivekananda's pithy statements:

"Coming and going is all pure delusion. The soul never comes nor goes. Where is the place to which it shall go when all space is in the soul? When shall be the time for entering and departing when all time is in the soul?" (Complete Works, vol. 5, p.68) Action requires time, space, and causation and therefore takes place only in relativity. Thus,

God is actionless. When the scriptures or realized beings claim that God is the only doer, this reveals their unity of vision where they see the one Reality manifesting as Intelligence, energy, and matter. They look within themselves and see body, energy, mind, intellect, and ego as mere containers for Consciousness (the Absolute) to manifest in and through. Seeing God in everything, as Sri Ramakrishna told the young Sharat (Swami Saradananda) is the highest realization possible in the world. Devotional disciplines, of either dualistic or qualified nondualistic schools, will also advise qualified practitioners to look upon themselves as vehicles for the manifestation of God. Such devotees must be very careful in this practice to avoid making God the scapegoat for their own selfish, desire-based whims. Sincerely practiced, this is a very rare and exacting discipline that requires the utmost integrity, discernment, and self-surrender.

Nature performs all action vs. only a Sentient agent can be the doer.

In the *Bhagavad Gita*, Sri Krishna affirms that the *Gunas* of *Prakriti* perform all action. *"When the seer perceives no agent other than the Gunas, and knows Him who is higher than the Gunas, he enters into My Being."* (Gita 14:19) Prakriti means nature, both unmanifested (potential) and manifested (what senses or mind can perceive). The three *gunas* are the warp and woof of manifestation: balance, activity, and inertia. When they are in equilibrium, Prakriti is unmanifested, and when they go out of equilibrium, the universe comes into manifestation via the cosmic principles (*tattvas*) they give rise to.

Thus, Nature performs all action and we are to be the unaffected Witness. When we are told that only a Sentient agent can be the doer, this means that Nature is insentient. Without a conscious Self associated with it, revealing it, and perceiving it, nothing can happen. This is all part of cosmology, *Sankhya*, which also states that all of nature exists for the benefit of the one conscious Self (*Purusha*, or *Atman*, in Vedanta). Speaking from the standpoint of qualified nondualism to resolve this apparent dichotomy: 1) For the Absolute/the Self/*Atman*, there is no action or agency, 2) nature creates the sense of agency via the ego and intellect, and, 3) the (apparent) union of the sentient Self and mind, etc., performs action with the *gunas* of *prakriti*.

"...the one intuitive into the nature of Guna and karma knows that Gunas as senses merely abide with Gunas as objects, and does not become entangled." Gita 3:28)

"He who, sitting like one unconcerned, is moved not by the Gunas, who, knowing that the Gunas operate, is firm and moves not..." (Gita 14:23)

Some Select Verses on Renunciation/Vairagyam
by Bhartrihari

Oh Siva! Have such places in the Himalayas become extinct,
That a man should go begging at others' doors?
Have the roots in the mountain forests all disappeared?
Have the springs all run dry?
Have the trees that bear sweet fruits all withered and fallen?
With bark for garments, the free will never again look with fear
Upon the face of those fools whose heads are turned by a little wealth.

Nevertheless, Arise! Let us return; Let us go back into the wilds,
Where pure roots and fruits will be our food,
Pure water our only drink, pure leaves our bed,
And where the small-minded, the thoughtless, of tiny intellect,
And those whose hearts are fixated with wealth, will not venture.

For, sitting to meditate on my stone seat in a mountain cave,
I can, with a secret smile on my lips, rejoice in inner freedom,
And be exceedingly glad that I am not one who compromises,
Nor settles contentedly into a life of base enjoyment of objects.

Like our ancestors before us, we have become attached to life-force,
And with it, have sung our glories about our empty and ignoble acts
Attaching ourselves stupidly to wealth, objects, and enjoyments,
We have only traced the trail of a fragile drop of water
Across the width of a swiftly withering Lotus leaf.

Not knowing the destructive power in flame, the insect falls into it.
The fish swallows the bait, not knowing about the hook inside.
Like that, though well aware of the vanity and dangers of the world,
Men nevertheless cannot give it up; such is the power of delusion.

But seeing that enjoyments are transitory, like high-breaking waves,
And that life is always susceptible to a speedy dissolution,
The wise teachers of men, minds resolved to benefit humanity,
Put forth their energies to help them reach the highest beatitude.

Seeing the varieties of allurements in nature, all transitory,
Cease to wander about aimlessly in this ever-changing world.
Place your faith in the words of the illumined souls, like your guru.
Then quell hope with its thousand meshes, and learn concentration.

Have you ever meditated perfectly on the Blessed Feet of the Lord?
Did you study the dharma diligently, and with it, reach high heaven?
Though loving your mother, and under her protection,
Did you not still became a sword to cut down her youth?
I ask you: what is there worthy of mention in a life such as this?

I will never again seek the transient, and the changeful.
Having discovered my own Atman, I have found my highest good.
The troublesome labyrinth of sense objects now beckons no more,
The mind-stream is no more agitated, its flux having been stilled.

When will that day come, when in a forest, awake all night,
My sense of time shall pass by in an ecstatic blur?
Then, a serpent and a garland the same, foe and friend the same,
A bed of flowers and a bed of stone, the same,
A beautiful woman and a blade of grass, the same,
I will chant intensely, Siva!, Hara!,
under the beams of an autumnal moon.

This Universe, I have seen, is only a tiny circle, and insubstantial.
What is there to desire in it except desire itself, albeit misguided?
After all, I muse: what is all this big deal about it and its activities?
Will the ocean break into waves by the jumping of a few fish?

Raja Yoga Correspondence Course

An in-depth study of Patanjali's Yoga Sutras with Babaji Bob Kindler.

Contact: srvinfo@srv.org

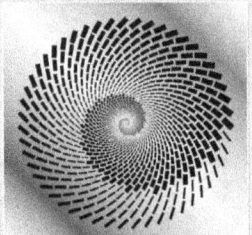

This meditative state is the highest state of existence. So long as there is desire, no real happiness can come.

It is only the contemplative, witness-like study of objects that brings to us real enjoyment and happiness. It is only to the soul that has attained to this contemplative state that the world really becomes beautiful.

To him who desires nothing, and does not mix himself up with them, the manifold changes of nature are one panorama of beauty and sublimity.

— Swami Vivekananda

A Ground-Breaking Interfaith Program

In the Spirit Interviews with Lex Hixon

From the early 1970's through the late 1980's, Lex Hixon hosted **In the Spirit** from WBAI, in NYC. As a list, the fruit of this selfless work reads like a comprehensive Who's Who of the spiritual, artistic and intellectual heart and mind of both Eastern and Western cultures. Over 300 programs can be downloaded at www.srv.org

- Kalu Rinpoche
- Sakya Trizin
- Dudjom Rinpoche
- Tartan Tulku
- Trungpa Rinpoche
- Bernie Glassman
- Master Shen Yen
- Rebbi Gedalia
- Rabbi Zalman Schachter
- Rabbi Dovid Din
- Sheikh Muzafer
- Guru Bawa
- Pir Vilayet Khan
- Swami Muktananda
- Meher Baba
- Sri Chinmoy
- Ram Das
- Swami Rama
- Mother Teresa
- Father Daniel Barrigan
- Programs on Meister Eckhart, Padre Pio, Mother Mary, Jesus Christ
- Programs on Sri Ramakrishna, Divine Mother, Ramana Maharishi, Sri Aurobindo

---

Hearing about Brahman is good.

Taking teachings on Brahman is better.

Meditating directly on Brahman is better still.

But best of all is that meditation in which all doubt about the nature of Reality dies away forever.

—Shankaracharya's *Crest Jewel of Discrimination*

Dharma Weekends at SRV Associations

Online & in-person with

Babaji Bob Kindler, Spiritual Director

Satsang
Join us for Q & A
Bring your questions from classes and studies

Saturdays at 8:00am HST
On Zoom

Brahman Bytes
Group Philosophical Discussion

Saturdays at 10:00am HST
On Zoom from community.srvwisdom.org

Sunday Class
Vedanta, Yoga, Tantra

Sundays at 2:30pm HST
On Zoom & in person

Schedule Subject to Change | Sign up for schedule emails: srv.org

SRV Associations 2022
Babaji's Teaching Schedule for the West Coast

Babaji Bob Kindler's Dharma Visits to Portland, OR

SRV Oregon
1922 S.E. 42nd Ave., Portland, OR 97215 | 808-990-3354 | srvinfo@srv.org

February, 2022

Winter Retreat at Windwood Waters
Continuing our study of the **Annapurna Upanisad**
Thursday, Feb 17 — Monday, Feb 21, 2022

Feb 25	Fri	7:00pm	**Satsang** in the ashram
Feb 26	Sat	9:30am	**Class** on Amrita Nada Upanisad
		6:00pm	**Sri Ramakrishna Puja**
Feb 27	Sun	9:30am	**Class** on Amrita Nada Upanisad

May, 2022

May 20	Fri	7:00pm	**Satsang** in the ashram
May 21	Sat	9:30am	**Class** on Amrita Nada Upanisad
		6:00pm	**SRV Puja**
May 22	Sun	9:30am	**Class** on Amrita Nada Upanisad

Suggested Donation for classes: $20. No one turned away.

Memorial Weekend Retreat at Windwood Waters
Dissolving the Mind Stream in Indian Traditions
Thursday, May 26th — Monday, May 30, 2022

August & September, 2022

Aug 26	Fri	7:00pm	**Satsang** in the ashram
Aug 27	Sat	9:30am	**Class**—TBA
		6:00pm	**SRV Puja**
Aug 28	Sun	9:30am	**Class**—TBA

Labor Day Weekend Retreat TBA
Thursday, September 1—Monday, September 5

Stay Informed about Weekly Classes, Retreats, Publications, & Online Seminars

Sign our email list & Explore SRV Offerings

We invite you to visit
SRV's Facebook & Instagram Pages:
Facebook.com/srvvedanta
Instagram.com/srvassociations

SRV Websites:
www.srv.org
community.SRVWisdom.org
www.nectarofnondualtruth.org

Explore Mother India's Timeless Wisdom

www.srv.org
- Sanskrit Chants to Learn & Practice
- "In the Spirit" Audio Interviews
- Teachings for Youth/Children
- Articles on SRV Ideals, Teachers, & Wisdom
- Sacred Books & Music online store
- This website is the hub for everything SRV....

Join the Ashram of the Subtle Realms:
community.SRVWisdom.org
- Spiritual Community
- Easy access to: live classes, archived video and audio classes
- Nectar of Non-Dual Truth back issues
- Special discounts for books, charts, and a retreat of your choice.

Nectar of Non-Dual Truth—A Journal of Universal Religious & Philosophical Teachings
www.nectarofnondualtruth.org
- Learn about Nectar's mission
- Preview upcoming articles and writers
- Order back issues

Dharma Art Wisdom Charts—For the Study of Wisdom
Dharmaartwisdomcharts.com
- Beautiful, essential Wisdom charts for Home, School, Spiritual Center, and Yoga Studios.
- Archival inks, ready to frame

YouTube Channel Class Series with Babaji Bob Kindler
Youtube.com/user/SRVAssociations
- Mother's Path of Nonduality
- God/Brahman Reflected in the Universe
- Non-Touch Yoga of Gaudapada
- The Third Eye & Kundalini's 7 Chakras
- Spiritual Interviews
- Satsangs, Sacred Music Videos, & more

Comments about Nectar from our Readers

"I have been meaning to write and express my thanks for the great issues of Nectar you have created. I know of no other magazine that is so interreligious in its presentation yet whose staff and leaders are so dedicated to their own ideal. It is really very inspiring."

Brahmacharyi Vedatma

"Nectar of Nondual Truth has reached us in Australia, and we find that the journal is simply incomparable, containing not only articles of many of the world's religions, but various other helpful perspectives as well. Your work has helped the 'outback' be up front in its spiritual views. Many thanks."

Samuel Laslo

"I very much appreciate your detailed presentation of Advaita Vedanta, Sri Ramakrishna, and Mother Kali. I hope it will reach a large number of American Citizens."

President Maharaj,
Ramakrishna Order
Swami Ranganathananda

"I'm dazzled by a tradition that truly acknowledges the deepest held truths held by different religions and I know that this is a rare thing. I am delighted to find the pearls of wisdom shared in this journal from other traditions such as Judaism, Sufism, Buddhism, Hinduism, Vedanta, Islam, etc., acknowledged and held high along with the truths of SRV's Tradition."

Sacred Music from Hawaii
Jai Ma Music
The Music of Babaji Bob Kindler

Chanting • Instrumental • Devotional • Poetry

Kali Bol Ramakrishna
Gita Govinda Mala
Hari Om Ramanam
Guru Bhajans
Jai Ho Vivekananda!
Siva! Siva!
Hymns to the Goddess
Shakti Bhajans
Deva Devi Svarupaya
Kali Bol
Sarada Ramakrishna Name
Hymns to the Master & Mother
108 Names of Sarada
Universal Aspects
Bhajananda
Avatar Bhajans
Puja/Arati Hymns
Wingspan
Music from the Matrix I
Music from the Matrix II
Waters of Life
Ever Free Never Bound
Tiger's Paw
Sound Castles
Worlds Unseen
Ecstatic Songs of Ramprasad I
Ecstatic Songs of Ramprasad II

Available at www.SRV.org

And your favorite streaming service.

Advaita-satya-amritam

NECTAR
Of Non-Dual Truth

Subscription Form
Order Next Issue by Feb. 15, 2023

Annual Subscription: $18 (U.S.)
Annual Subscription: $20 (International)
Nectar is mailed out once each year in the Spring

Subscribe online: www.srv.org > Nectar Journal > Subscribe
Scan this QR code and you will be right there!

Or, Subscribe by check:
Please fill out the back side of this form and mail it with your check to:
SRV Associations, PO Box 1364, Honokaa, HI 96727 (*payable to: SRV Associations*)
MasterCard or Visa accepted via phone as well:
808-990-3354 • srvinfo@srv.org • www.srv.org

#37

Advaita-satya-amritam

NECTAR
Of Non-Dual Truth

Subscription Form
Order Next Issue by Feb. 15, 2023

Annual Subscription: $18 (U.S.)
Annual Subscription: $20 (International)
Nectar is mailed out once each year in the Spring

Subscribe online: www.srv.org > Nectar Journal > Subscribe
Scan this QR code and you will be right there!

Or, Subscribe by check:
Please fill out the back side of this form and mail it with your check to:
SRV Associations, PO Box 1364, Honokaa, HI 96727 (*payable to: SRV Associations*)
MasterCard or Visa accepted via phone as well:
808-990-3354 • srvinfo@srv.org • www.srv.org

#37

Advaita-satya-amritam

NECTAR
Of Non-Dual Truth

Subscription Form
Order Next Issue by Feb. 15, 2023

Annual Subscription: $18 (U.S.)
Annual Subscription: $20 (International)
Nectar is mailed out once each year in the Spring

Subscribe online: www.srv.org > Nectar Journal > Subscribe
Scan this QR code and you will be right there!

Or, Subscribe by check:
Please fill out the back side of this form and mail it with your check to:
SRV Associations, PO Box 1364, Honokaa, HI 96727 (*payable to: SRV Associations*)
MasterCard or Visa accepted via phone as well:
808-990-3354 • srvinfo@srv.org • www.srv.org

#37

Your Shipping information: (if subscribing by mail)

Name: _____

Address: _____

City, State, Zip: _____

Email: _____

You Can Help Others Receive Nectar.   Your gift is tax-deductible.

We continue to supply free copies to prison inmates, religious organizations, and persons requiring financial assistance. You can help bridge the financial gap with a separate donation to Nectar. You will receive both our sincere gratitude and a donation letter for your taxes. SRV Associations is a 501c3 tax exempt religious organization.

MasterCard or Visa accepted online at www.srv.org > Giving
Or you can pay by credit card over the phone.
808-990-3354 • srvinfo@srv.org • www.srv.org • Questions? Call or write us!

Your Shipping information: (if subscribing by mail)

Name: _____

Address: _____

City, State, Zip: _____

Email: _____

You Can Help Others Receive Nectar.   Your gift is tax-deductible.

We continue to supply free copies to prison inmates, religious organizations, and persons requiring financial assistance. You can help bridge the financial gap with a separate donation to Nectar. You will receive both our sincere gratitude and a donation letter for your taxes. SRV Associations is a 501c3 tax exempt religious organization.

MasterCard or Visa accepted online at www.srv.org > Giving
Or you can pay by credit card over the phone.
808-990-3354 • srvinfo@srv.org • www.srv.org • Questions? Call or write us!

Your Shipping information: (if subscribing by mail)

Name: _____

Address: _____

City, State, Zip: _____

Email: _____

You Can Help Others Receive Nectar.   Your gift is tax-deductible.

We continue to supply free copies to prison inmates, religious organizations, and persons requiring financial assistance. You can help bridge the financial gap with a separate donation to Nectar. You will receive both our sincere gratitude and a donation letter for your taxes. SRV Associations is a 501c3 tax exempt religious organization.

MasterCard or Visa accepted online at www.srv.org > Giving
Or you can pay by credit card over the phone.
808-990-3354 • srvinfo@srv.org • www.srv.org • Questions? Call or write us!

www.ingramcontent.com/pod-product-compliance
Lightning Source LLC
Chambersburg PA
CBHW081402080526
44588CB00016B/2572